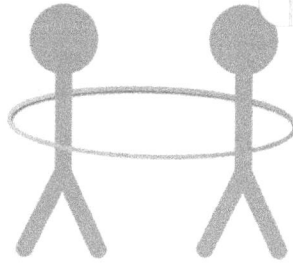

Sharing Lives

SHARING LIVES

Course book

A course to help Christians share their lives with Muslims

Bert de Ruiter

EEA
EUROPEAN EVANGELICAL ALLIANCE

VTR
Publications

„Sharing Lives" ist Teil von Operation Mobilisation.
http://www.sharinglives.eu

Bibliographic information published by the Deutsche Nationalbibliothek
The Deutsche Nationalbibliothek lists this publication in the Deutsche
Nationalbibliografie; detailed bibliographic data are available on the
Internet at http://dnb.dnb.de .

ISBN 978-3-95776-202-3 (VTR)
ISBN 978-3-902669-26-1 (OM)

VTR Publications, Gogolstr. 33, 90475 Nürnberg, Germany
http://www.vtr-online.com

The contact details of your local OM office you find at
http://www.om.org

Scripture quotations taken from The Holy Bible,
New International Version (1995).

INTRODUCTION

Throughout Europe Christians and Muslims live in close proximity to each other. They pass each other in the streets, stand next to each other waiting for the bus, or share apartment buildings, classrooms and business canteens. Unfortunately, they are essentially strangers to each other.

What is it that hinders Christians from sharing their lives with Muslims? One doesn't have to fly across the world to meet Muslims, but only has to cross the street. What keeps people from doing so? Is it lack of information? It does not seem like it. There are plenty of good books on Islam, and many schools offer seminars and courses on Islam.

Meanwhile, Islam is "hot" in today's media. Many Christians talk about the Muslims who burn churches, persecute Christians, fly airplanes into buildings, and hijack people in different parts of the world. For a long time these events occurred far away. But then trains were bombed by Muslims in Europe, and a Dutch television producer was killed by a Moroccan in Amsterdam. Also, some Christians point out that there are Muslims who seem reluctant to adapt to European values, seeking instead the right to apply their own (Sharia) law in the countries where they have come to settle in Europe.

Research has shown that fear is the single most significant factor preventing Christians from relating to Muslims.

The course *Sharing Lives* has been developed to help Christians in Europe overcome their negative attitudes: fear of Islam and Muslims, as well as their prejudice and suspicion regarding Islam and Muslims. This course is intended to help Christians learn to respond with grace in order that they might share their lives with Muslims.

The name of the course is taken from 1 Thessalonians 2:8, where the Apostle Paul writes: *"We loved you so much that we were delighted to share with you not only the gospel but our lives as well, because you had become so dear to us."*

This verse is an example of what it means to be an incarnational witness: whereby sharing the Gospel and sharing lives are integrated.

The main objective of the course *Sharing Lives* is to help Christians change their attitude towards Islam and Muslims, from one of fear to one of grace; and to encourage them to develop meaningful relationships with Muslims in their neighbourhood, in order that they might share their lives and the Gospel of Jesus Christ with them.

The course intends to encourage Christians to share their lives with Muslims in five steps. Each step is addressed in one lesson:

Lesson 1: Our view of Islam and Muslims
Lesson 2: Developing an attitude of grace
Lesson 3: Understanding Muslims
Lesson 4: Meeting with Muslims
Lesson 5: Developing relationships that last

In addition to this course handbook there is a trainer's handbook and other resources that can be used during the course (e.g. power-point presentations and film clips). And further information can be found on the website www.sharinglives.eu.

Dr. Bert de Ruiter
Amsterdam

LESSON 1:
OUR VIEW OF ISLAM

Aim: To enable participants to reflect on their attitudes towards Islam and Muslims in light of Scripture.

> **Take the worksheet and answer the following questions:**
>
> **What words, images, pictures and thoughts come to mind when you think of Islam and Muslims?**
> **Finish the following sentence:**
> **"When it comes to Islam, I think that in 20 years' time … ."**
> **Finish the following sentence:**
> **"When it comes to Islam, I would like that … ."**
> **Discuss the responses that each person has given.**

1   God's calling

In Matthew 28:18-20 we read the following words of the risen Lord Jesus Christ to his apostles:

"All authority in heaven and on earth has been given to me. Therefore go and make disciples of all nations, baptizing them in the name of the Father and of the Son and of the Holy Spirit, and teaching them to obey everything I have commanded you. And surely I am with you always, to the very end of the age."

This Great Commission is still relevant today. The Lord Jesus Christ still wants to make all peoples of the earth into his disciples. This includes the Muslim in our country, city and neighborhood. The Lord of the Church calls the members of the church to make disciples of all people.

Through the ages He has used His people to draw others to Himself. But sometimes he had to deal with unwilling workers, as we see in the life of Jonah.

2   Jonah's response to God's calling

The word of the Lord came to Jonah son of Amittai: "Go to the great city of Nineveh, and preach against it, because its wickedness has come up before me." But Jonah ran away from the Lord. (Jnh. 1:1-3)

In the book of Jonah we learn about God's compassion for the world, even for the enemies of Israel. God knew the people of Nineveh and what they had done. They deserved his judgment and punishment for their sins. But instead of punishing them straight away, he wanted to give them an opportunity to repent, so He could forgive them. God has more pleasure in forgiving than in punishing. We often see that God wants to use his children to carry out his purposes for this world.

Also in this story we learn that God wants to use Jonah to carry out his purposes for Nineveh. But we also see that Jonah was unwilling to fulfill this task.

In order for us to understand what God's calling of Jonah meant, it helps us to learn more about Nineveh.

a   Background on Assyria and Nineveh

In Genesis 10:8-11, we read that Nineveh was built by Nimrod, one of the first mighty warriors on earth. In Jonah's day Nineveh was the capital of the Assyrian empire. Assyria was a kingdom between the Tigris and Euphrates rivers that dominated the ancient world from the ninth century to the seventh century BC. The empire was one of the best fighting machines of the ancient world and one of the most bloodthirsty and cruel civilizations ever known.

Terror was one factor contributing greatly to Assyrian success. Theirs was a calculated policy of terror, possibly the earliest example of organized psychological warfare.

It was not unusual for them to kill every man, woman, and child in captured cities. Assyria became a byword for cruelty and atrocity. They skinned their prisoners alive, and cut off various body parts to inspire terror in their enemies.

In their monuments and reports of history they brag about how high the pyramids of human heads were which they built from their conquered foes and how they burned cities and impaled human beings and cut off hands and flayed bodies and so on. One of the ancient monuments discovered in the ruins of ancient Assyria bears this inscription by King Asshurizirpal (whose reign began in 883 BC.) regarding a conquered city:

"Their men, young and old, I took as prisoners. Of some I cut off the feet and hands; of others I cut off the noses, ears, and lips; of the young men's ears I made a heap; of the old men's heads I built a minaret." Hawlinson's "Five Great Monarchies" vol. 2, p. 85.

Assyrian policy was to deport conquered peoples to other lands within the empire, to destroy their sense of nationalism, and break any pride or hope of rebellion and replace them with strangers from far away.

This is what they did with the northern part of Israel in 722 BC. In 2 Ki. 17:24 we read:

"The king of Assyria brought people from Babylon, Cuthah, Avva, Harnath and Sepharvaim and settled them in the towns of Samaria to replace the Israelites."

These people came to be called 'the Samaritans'.

In Nahum 3:1-4 – an account from 150 years after Jonah, we read the following description of Nineveh:

"… the city of blood, full of lies, full of plunder, never without victims…"

It also speaks about the city's sorceries and witchcraft. The pagan worship of the Assyrians was vehemently condemned by several prophets of the Old Testament (see Is. 10:5; Eze. 16:28; Hos. 8.9).

Against this background it is not hard to understand that most people of Israel looked at the Assyrians with deep-seated hatred, suspicion and fear. We also begin to understand Jonah's reluctance to go to these people.

> **To discuss:**
> **Try to put yourself in Jonah's shoes. How would you have respond-**
> **ed to God's calling?**
> **Are we still suffering of the "Jonah syndrome" today? If so, in**
> **what way?**

3   Islam: our Nineveh?

The fearful Assyrian empire is gone. The famous city of Nineveh is just a small village in present-day Iraq. Other powers and authorities, cities and people have taken their place. For many Christians in Europe their contemporary 'Nineveh' is Islam. They see the aggression of Muslim extremists, hear how Islamic spiritual leaders say things that fill them with fear, and they look with suspicion to the many Muslims that have come to live in our countries. One of the biggest obstacles for Christians to overcome in order to be able to share their lives with Muslims is their own attitude.
The attitude of many Christians in Europe towards Islam and Muslims is one of fear, prejudice and suspicion.

4   Dealing with our fear of Islam

Fear is a natural, basic element and instinct of our human nature. It is an emotion that is created by God. Fear can function as a warning light when danger is near. A healthy fear protects us from real danger. Not all fear is sinful, e.g. Jesus expressed fear in the Garden of Geth-semane. However, not all perceived danger is real danger.

A much used acronym for fear is:

> **F**alse
> **E**vidence
> **A**ppearing
> **R**eal

All fear is based on perception. Although a vast majority of the things we fear never become reality, the false evidence is sometimes very convincing!

Fear often distorts our sense of reality. Fear distorts our perception of ourselves so that we seem weaker than we really are. It distorts the size of our problems, or the strength of those we believe to be our enemies, so that they seem huge and undefeatable. But perhaps most significantly, fear distorts our picture of God. God seems weak, uninvolved, or uncaring in the midst of our troubles.

The difference between a legitimate fear of a dangerous world and a fear that imprisons us and even offends God has to do with *what* or *whom* we fear and where that fear drives us. Does it drive us to protect ourselves, or does it drive us to God, our Protector? Proverbs 29:25 tells us that *"Fear of man will prove to be a snare, but whoever trusts in the Lord is kept safe."*

Fear can become a weapon of Satan, who uses our instinct of fear to hinder us from becoming all that God wants us to be and to do. The command, "fear not" is one of the most frequently-repeated commands in all of Scripture, an indication that fear and anxiety are not only part of the most common human condition, but also an emotion or reaction to life that is least warranted for a follower of Christ.
David describes this paradox beautifully, when he writes:

"When I am afraid, I will trust in you. In God, whose word I praise, in God I trust; I will not be afraid. What can mortal man do to me?" (Ps. 56:3, 4)

One way to deal with our fear is to learn more about what causes this fear.

In the context of this course, when we deal with our fear of Islam, it is good to learn more about how Muslims practice their faith, and interpret the Qur'an and how Islam is developing in Europe. We will look at this in more detail in lesson 3 of this course.

Another important step to deal with our fear is to take it seriously:

"When our sight is blurred by the effects of fear, how do we get our orientation back? How do we regain a sense of reality when the threats seem so real and the dangers so present? The answer boils down to feel fear. If you avoid your fear, it will turn dark and destructive. Instead, allowing it to stalk you without trying to wave it away by reciting pious platitudes or distracting yourself in busyness. Fear faced is a heart exposed. Fear clarifies by exposing who (and what) we serve. It can be classified in two categories: fear of the world and fear of God."[1]

Most of our fears arise out of our demand to gain a degree of pleasure, honor, meaning, security and joy in a world that more often hands us pain, shame, chaos, and sorrow. The fear of the world is another way of describing the fear of what life – of what others – may do to us.

Another way to deal with fear in our lives is to put that which causes us fear into the context of another reality. As a Christian this reality is: our God, our Creator and our Father in Christ Jesus. One of the ways to overcome fear of men and circumstances is to become more aware of who God is.

This is one of the messages of Isaiah 40-54, which deals with a time in the history of God's people that might have some parallels with our time.

---

[1] Dan. B. Allender & Tremper Longman III, *The Cry of the Soul, how our emotions reveal our deepest questions, about God* (Colorado Springs: NavPress, 1994), 99.

5   Background to Isaiah 40-54

The prophet Isaiah prophesied in a time that turned out to be one of the blackest periods in the history of the people of Israel. The northern kingdom (10 tribes) was deported to Assyria and the southern Kingdom (2 tribes) was about to experience the same, being taken and held captive by another world power: Babylon.

In Isaiah chapters 40 through 54 we find words of God spoken to His people about a difficult period in their history. They were in exile and the temple and the holy city of Jerusalem were destroyed. The people were scattered across foreign nations. Other kings and powers, empires and their gods had overtaken them.

Gone were all the glorious days of the past. No temple, no country, no identity. The people were discouraged, disheartened and thought that God had abandoned them. They said to each other:

"My way is hidden from the Lord; my cause is disregarded by my God."(Is. 40:27)

and also:

"The Lord has forsaken me, the Lord has forgotten me." (Is. 49:14).

The glorious days of David and Solomon had ended. Israel was no longer an independent kingdom. They had imagined that as long as the temple were to remain in Jerusalem, they would be safe. But now the temple had been destroyed. The people are described as *"a people plundered and looted, all of them trapped in pits or hidden away in prisons. They have become plunder, with no one to rescue them; they have been made loot, with no one to say: 'Send them back'."* (Is. 42:22; cf 49:19-21)

They were disappointed in God, believing God did not see them, believing that he did not know and does not care. Gradually they became convinced that God wasn't able to do anything about it. They didn't expect anything from God anymore. Their singing of the old days was over. Psalm 137 expresses their feelings during this time.

"By the rivers of Babylon we sat and wept when we remembered Zion. There on the poplars we hung our harps, for there our captors asked us for songs, our tormentors demanded songs of joy; they said, 'Sing us one of the songs of Zion!' 'How can we sing the songs of the Lord while in a foreign land?'" (137:1-4).

The people were convinced that the power of God was limited to the borders of the Promised Land.

They were discouraged, depressed, insecure and afraid.

For this dark time of Israel's history, God gave the prophet Isaiah a word to comfort them (Is. 40:1) and in doing so, he regularly tells them 'not to fear' (e.g. 40:9; 41:10, 13, 14; 43:1, 5; 44:2, 8; 51:7, 12; 54:4, 14).

God wants to help His people overcome their fear, by pointing them to Himself:

"... do not be afraid; say ... Here is your God." (Is. 40:9).

God comforts his fearful people by revealing more of Himself:

"I, even I, am he who comforts you. Who are you that you fear ... that you forget the Lord your Maker ... that you live in constant terror every day ..." (Is. 51:12, 13).

From the part of the Bible which starts with the words: "Comfort, comfort my people, says your God" (40:1) and ends with the words "No weapon forged against you will prevail, and you will refute every tongue that accuses you. This is the heritage of the servants of the Lord, and this is their vindication from me." (54:17), we can note five aspects of God that can help us deal with our fear of Islam:

A   God promises to be with us – no matter what

"Do not be afraid for I am with you." (Is. 43:5; cf. Is. 41:10)

One of the reasons people of God should not fear, regardless of the circumstances, is because God has promised to be present with them.

God will be with us (41:10; 43:5), He will not forsake us (41:17; 42:16) and He will not forget us (44:21; 49:15).

This is not a guarantee for a trouble free life. There may be trials and difficulties, but nothing can really hurt us: *"Fear not … when you pass through the waters, I will be with you." (Is. 43:2)* God's presence comforts us in fearful circumstances.

B   God's plans prevails – no matter what

"I make known the end from the beginning, from ancient times, what is still to come. I say: My purpose will stand, and I will do all that I please … . What I have said, that will I bring about; what I have planned, that will I do." (Is. 46:10, 11)

In his desire to comfort his people and to help them subdue their fears, God wants them to focus on who He is:

B.1   He is the Sovereign Creator

"I, even I, am he who comforts you. Who are you that you fear mortal men, the sons of men, who are but grass, that you forget the Lord your Maker, who stretched out the heavens and laid the foundations of the earth, that you live in constant terror every day, because of the wrath of the oppressor?" (Is. 51:12, 13)

In fearful times, when it storms around us, when the foundations of our life seem to fall from underneath us, God wants us to remember that He is our Sovereign Creator. Our God is the only Creator of all things (44:24; 48:13; 51:16). He weighs and measures (40:12) heaven and earth, waters and mountains (40:12), forests and animals (40:16); stars and planets (40:26) and also nations and islands (40:15). It is the Sovereign Creator who gives breath to its people and life to all who walk on planet earth (42:5).

Rulers and all people of the earth owe their existence to the everlasting God, the Creator of the ends of the earth (40:28).

He created the heavens and the earth for a purpose (45:18). He is the Sovereign Creator, who doesn't need help from anyone (40:13, 14; 44:24). We can trust His power, wisdom and purpose, even if we don't always understand it.

People and powers that look impressive to us and that cause us fear are just like a drop in a bucket (40:15) or grasshoppers (40:22), or clay (45:9) in the hands of the Sovereign Creator.

B.2   He is the Judge of all the earth

"Be silent before me, you islands! Let the nations renew their strength! Let them come forward and speak; let us meet together at the place of judgment."(Is. 41:1)

God calls the nations and their idols to present their case and set forth their arguments (Is. 41:19-25) and to bring in their witnesses (43:9-21), to gather together and assemble (45:20). Isaiah gives us a picture of our righteous God calling all nations, all the peoples to gird up their strength and come before him for judgment. God is the judge of all the earth. He calls all nations to give an account of their lives and their religions and their thoughts. They come into his courtroom. He is the judge of all and in His proper time, He will pass sentence on every person.

He is committed to justice and righteousness. His justice will become a light to the nations (51:5) and his arm will bring justice to the nations (51:5) and his righteousness will never fail (51:6). Even if injustice or unrighteousness seems to rule now, God, the Judge of all the earth, will set things straight in his time and there will come a time when every knee will bow before him and every tongue will confess His Lordship (45:23).

An assurance of God's judgment at the end of this system of things enables us to refrain from taking matters into our own hands in the middle of it.

B.3   He is the Ruler of all rulers

"Who has aroused one from the east whom He [God] calls in right-eousness to His feet? He delivers up nations before him, and subdues kings. He makes them like dust with his sword, as the wind-driven chaff with his bow." (Is. 41:2, 3)

God humbles and brings to nothing the princes and rulers that look so impressive and that presently cause so much harm (40:23). He uses political leaders, who think they are carrying out their own plans, to fulfill His eternal purposes (41:25 cf; 44:28; 45:1-13).

The passages in Isaiah primarily refer to Cyrus the Persian king, whom God calls 'my shepherd' and 'my anointed', who will accomplish all that God pleases (44:28 and 45:1).

We get a picture of God rousing a king, leading him in conquest and delivering up nations before him. God is Ruler of the rulers of history. He controls the affairs of men and nations for his purposes. God will make an end to the evil empires of this world (e.g. Babylon in Isaiah's time), despite the fact that they think their power lasts forever (47:7). In his sovereignty, God used foreign nations to chastise Israel (47:6).

B.4   He is the First and the Last

"Who has performed and accomplished it, calling forth the genera-tions from the beginning? I, the Lord, am the first, and with the last. I am He." (Is. 41:4; cf. 43:10; 44:6; 48:12)

God is in control of the course of human events. God is the first – he is the absolute reality before all other realities and on which all other realities depend. He is the uncreated first. He is eternal (40:28). And he will be there with the last when all is accomplished according to his eternal purpose. He knows the end from the beginning (44:7; 46:10; 48:3). He knows the future (45:11).

Human history is not merely a random, meaningless combination of undirected events. There is a God in heaven who directs human events towards a final resolution and fulfillment.

This means that God absolutely *has* a plan for human history, and He directs the path of human events toward His designed fulfillment.

If God is both the first and the last, then He also has authority over everything in between. It is He who directs all of human history and even our individual lives.

The fact that God calls Himself the First and the Last also means that He is the only real power, the only real authority. The Ultimate reality, the Only Savior: *I, even I, am the Lord, and apart from me there is no savior.* (43:11, also 44:8; 44:24; 45:5, 6, 18, 21, 22; 46:9, 10).

Jesus takes the same title of the First and the Last in Revelation 1:17 and 22:13.

To discuss:

- **God is the sovereign Lord of history. What does this teach us about the establishment of Islam in the 6th century AD?**
- **In light of God's sovereignty how should we view fundamentalist Muslims, and groups like the Taliban and Al-Qaeda? Could these people and groups be used by God to carry out His purposes? If so, what purposes might these be?**
- **What is the relationship between the sovereignty of God and the arrival of millions of Muslims to Europe? In discussing this, consider what the Apostle Paul said: "God determined the exact places where humankind should live ... so they may reach out for Him and find Him (Ac. 17:26-27).**

C   **God is committed to His people – no matter what**

"But you [are] Israel, My servant, Jacob whom I have chosen, descendant of Abraham My friend, you whom I have taken from the ends of the earth, and called from its remotest parts, and said to you, 'You are My servant, I have chosen you and not rejected you." (Is. 41:8, 9)

"Fear not, for I have redeemed you; I have summoned you by name; you are mine." (Is. 43:1)

In the time addressed by Isaiah, God's people thought it was over. Other powers seemed stronger while their own future seemed bleak. In our time, many Christians in Europe fear that the church in Europe will disappear and that Islam will take over. They see churches being converted to mosques and they feel that the influence of Christianity in society is dwindling. Against this background Isaiah's words are still relevant. Isaiah points out to God's people of that time (and thus indirectly to the Christians of the 21st Century in Europe) that they are precious in his eyes (43:4); they are engraved on the palms of his hands (49:16).

God is not ashamed to call Himself their God (40:1; 43:3), their Savior (43:3), Redeemer (43:14), and King (43:15). He has tied his reputation to them (48:11; 43:7). He protects them in times of danger (43:2; 54:17); He guides them like a shepherd (40:11); He offers them His help (40:13, 14); He strengthens them (41:10). He comforts them (40:1; 51:12); He promises them a bright future (42:14-16; 43:5, 6).

D   God's purposes for his servants involves the cross
**   – no matter what**

God's promise to be with us; His sovereignty and commitment to us; these things do not mean that His people will not experience hard times, persecution and suffering.
On the contrary, in this part of Isaiah we learn that suffering is inseparable from the fulfillment of God's eternal purposes. In these chapters of Isaiah, we find four 'Servant Songs' (42:1-9; 49:1-6, 50:4-9, 52:13-53:12). Each passage speaks of a Servant figure that is given a mission by the Lord. The great work of the Lord on behalf of Israel, and on behalf of the entire world, that is spoken of in Isaiah is accomplished through the work of this figure. The character and ministry of this Servant of the Lord is fulfilled by Jesus. The Servant of the Lord surfaces as the figure that brings about the return from exile, which turns out to be not simply a geographical return but a spiritual return. It is through this Servant that God's purposes will be accomplished. It is not without significance that three of the four Servant Songs, speak of suffering. In the 2nd (49:4, 7) and the 3rd (50:6) it is not so prominent,

but in the 4th suffering plays a prominent role. If the Servant of the Lord could not avoid suffering on his road to glory and in accomplishing God's purposes, it seems that pain, suffering and persecution are normal aspects of following Jesus. This self-giving love of Jesus for His people is a model for one's relationships with Muslims.

6   The fear of the Lord to overcome fear

Who among you fears the Lord and obeys the word of his servant? Let him who walks in the dark, who has no light, trust in the name of the Lord and rely on his God. (Is. 50:10)

In this part of the Bible, where the Lord comforts his fearful people by pointing them to Himself, he exhorts them more than ten times 'to fear not'. We are encouraged to not fear: men, rulers, situations, our future, injustice, etc. But we do find encouragement to fear in one way, namely 'to fear the Lord'. Big fears make little fears go away. God is the One we should fear most of all. The expression 'fear of God' points to an attitude of respect, trust, submission and obedience. To fear God is to be consumed with His presence.

> "When we disorient ourselves by being less afraid of God than something else, we get into trouble. When we fear something else, we forget about fearing God. ... In God's presence, all human fears disappear like smoke dispersed by the wind. ... The fear of God does not drive us away from God, but rather to God. It is only as the fear of God overcomes our fear of the world that we can truly and productively cope with our fears in the world."[2]

The more one fears the Lord the less one fears men and circumstances. Fear of the Lord helps us to overcome fear of men, as David points out in Psalm 112:

"Blessed is the man who fears the Lord ... he will have no fear of bad news ... his heart is secure, he will have no fear ..." (Ps. 112:1, 7)

---

[2] Allender and Tremper Longman III, 102, 103.

Homework

The main homework to be taken from this lesson and in preparation for the next is: PRAYER, particularly prayer for change. Change in the world of Islam in general and change in our hearts in relationship to Muslims in particular. We want to encourage you to pray daily for Muslims. This can be for Muslims who are in the news, or people you have heard of or know personally. Pray that God will make them into His disciples.

1. Examine your life (ask God to help you see blind spots): are there areas in your life in which fear of men or circumstances exceeds your fear of God? How can you apply the lessons from Isaiah 40-55 to these situations?

2. We also want to encourage you to examine your attitude towards Islam and Muslims during your time of prayer. To make this as practical as possible, we suggest that you take the paper that you used at the beginning of this lesson, on which you wrote your thoughts and images about Islam and Muslims and how you anticipate or would like Islam to be in the next 20 years.

Use the content of this paper during your time of prayer until the next lesson in connection with reading the following Psalms:

Day 1: Psalm 137
Day 2: Psalm 109
Day 3: Psalm 55
Day 4: Psalm 69
Day 5: Psalm 56
Day 6: Psalm 27
Day 7: Psalm 91

Answer for each Psalm: what lesson from this Psalm can I apply to my attitude towards and my view of Muslims and Islam?

Some of these Psalms are so-called 'imprecatory Psalms', in which the writer asks God to punish his enemies. Many Christians find it difficult to see how these Psalms can be in harmony with, or in any way be consistent with God's love and His commandment to love our enemies. But this is not a contradiction. To pray these Psalms means that we acknowledge the truth of Romans 12:19-21 (quoting Deuteronomy 32:35) namely:

"Do not repay anyone evil for evil. Be careful to do what is right in the eyes of everybody. If it is possible, as far as it depends on you, live at peace with everyone. Do not take revenge, my friends, but leave room for God's wrath, for it is written: "It is mine to avenge; I will repay," says the Lord."

These Psalms teach us that in our interaction with our heavenly Father, there is room for our emotions, even negative emotions. When we bring our anger, fear, anxiety, and prejudice before a loving, gracious, holy and righteous God, our negative feelings can come to rest in His presence and He can teach us what it means to be gracious and forgiving, just like He is.

Psalm 137

This Psalm expresses the post-traumatic feelings of God's people, exiled in Babylon. They have experienced terrible violence, and they have been removed from their home and forced to live under an alien regime. They are full of grief and despair. They want to know what God is going to do about it. They want justice and revenge.

> "Daring to express a desire for revenge in the context of worship of the God who is love can lead to the agonized realization that the 'dashing against the rock' of any baby would be unbearable."[3]

Psalm 109

In this Psalm we listen to the voice of David who was full of anger about unjust assault. He was angry. He wanted vengeance – payment that extended to the entire family of the man who harmed him. He

---

[3] Ida Glaser: 'We Sat Down and Wept': Biblical Babylon and Israel as Resources for Conflict Situations, *The Round Table*, Vol 94, No. 382, 641-651, October 2005.

desires to see harm return to those whose assault has brought him agony. Reflect about the place of anger in a Christian's life.

Psalm 55

In this Psalm David expresses his great anxiety and fear. The danger that confronts him has seized his mind with such obsessive fury that he can think of nothing else. A close friend had violated David's trust and hurt him badly. David's desire is to flee far away from danger. But according to the final part of this psalm, he doesn't flee to the wilderness, but to God. David knows that God will respond to his fears by His divine presence.

Psalm 69

In the Psalms we encounter divine goodness in the midst of pain. Psalm 69 provides a good example of a transition from suffering, fear and anger to glory and rest. Because David's vision moves from his suffering to God, there is an abrupt change of mood at the end – from pain to joy (verses 30-36).

Psalm 56

This is another Psalm in which David brings his fear before the Lord. The Psalm expresses a paradox: "When I am afraid, I will trust in you … in God I trust, I will not be afraid." Do you recognize this paradox in your life?

Psalm 27

In this Psalm David acknowledges that God is bigger than his fearful circumstances. The circumstances may not change, but in God's presence one can have peace in the midst of trying circumstances.

Psalm 91

This Psalm teaches that in times of danger, when difficult circumstances and evil people challenge us, we can hide in the presence of God.

LESSON 2:
DEVELOPING AN ATTITUDE OF GRACE

Aim: to help participants understand the importance of the grace of God in the Bible and in our own lives, particularly in connection with Islam and Muslims

> **To do:**
> **Discuss with each other the homework of lesson 1.**
> **What did you learn?**

1   Introduction

In lesson 1 we have reflected on our attitude towards Islam and Muslims. When we bring our negative feelings of fear, prejudice and anxiety before the Lord, there is the potential to develop another attitude, namely one of grace, the subject of this second lesson. We want to reflect on the grace of God in the life of Jonah, and his reluctance to be a channel of that grace.

We would like to help you grow in understanding the importance of grace in the Bible and in our lives and we would like to explain what an attitude of grace towards Muslims looks like.

> **To do:**
> **Take a piece of paper and write down your description of 'grace'.**
>
> **To discuss:**
> **C.S. Lewis once said:**
> *Christianity's unique feature among world religions is grace.*
> *Do you agree with this? Explain your answer.*

2   Lessons in grace from the life of Jonah

"From inside the fish Jonah prayed to the Lord his God. He said: In my distress, I called to the Lord, and he answered me. From the depths of the grave, I called for help, and you listened to my cry." (Jnh. 2:1, 2)

Jonah had run away from the Lord, he was under God's judgment. Despite this, he prays to God for help. And the Lord answers him graciously. While in the fish, Jonah realizes his dependence upon the grace of God, and he cries: "Salvation comes from the Lord." (2:9). The fish symbolizes the grace of God in Jonah's life. We, who know this story of Jonah very well, often are blind to the scope of God's grace and compassion that we see here. The Lord wants to teach us to be gracious instead of proud and judgmental. He wants our hearts to be as wide in compassion as is His own. In the story of Jonah, however, we learn that Jonah had not yet grasped this lesson.

"O Lord, is this not what I said when I was still at home? That is why I was so quick to flee to Tarshish. I knew that you are a gracious and compassionate God, slow to anger and abounding in love, a God who relents from sending calamity." (Jnh. 4:1, 2)

What Jonah suspected and the reason why he disobeyed God's calling to go to Nineveh, becomes reality: God forgives the people of Nineveh and shows them grace instead of judgment. In chapter 4 of this book we learn about God's love and patience with Jonah. God isn't satisfied with mere compliance, which is what he got from Jonah in chapter 3 when Jonah had preached judgment. What God wants is for Jonah to learn to be gracious to those people to whom God is Himself gracious. Jonah's heart has not changed since his original call in chapter 1.

God asks Jonah "Have you any right to be angry?" (4:4) God is calling Jonah to examine himself and his attitude towards the people among which God had called him to minister. Although Jonah makes a beautiful theological statement (in 4:2), the rest of the chapter shows that good theology does not automatically lead to a state of mind and an attitude of the heart that are in agreement with it. Therefore Jonah is asked to examine himself.

Think about it: If anybody has a right to be angry with the Ninevites it is God, who hates sin and violence. And yet he chose to offer grace and forgiveness to sinners and violent people. God's question implies: who is Jonah that he is angry when God chooses not to destroy Nineveh? Jonah knows that it says in the Pentateuch, "Vengeance is mine and recompense" (Dt. 32:35). That is God's responsibility, not Jonah's. Jonah's problem is that he wants to control God.

We play God when we continue to be angry at individuals or groups of people whom God has forgiven, when we take their punishment into our own hands through a negative attitude, vindictive words, or even hostile, destructive actions. We are running ahead of God in meting out what we think justice demands. God asks us just as he asked Jonah, "Is that your right?" And the only correct answer should be: "No, Lord, it is your right, not mine. I don't do well to be angry." Those who benefit from God's compassion have no right to complain against the sovereign extension of mercy to others, no matter how undeserving they may seem.

> **To discuss:**
> **It was very hard for Jonah to be a 'Grace-giver'. Do you recognize this in yourself? In what situations do you find it hard to approach others with grace?**

3   A description of grace

"... by the grace of God I am what I am ..." (1 Co. 15:9-11)

Someone has devised the following acronym, which is not a bad "definition" of grace:

God's **R**iches **A**t **C**hrist's **E**xpense

One of the most familiar short definitions of grace is "God's unmerited favor." The Greek word for grace is charis. Its basic idea is simply "non-meritorious or unearned favor, an unearned gift, a favor or blessings bestowed as a gift, freely and never as merit for work performed." The Hebrew term used for 'grace' means 'to bend, to stoop'. It includes the idea of 'condescending favor' (Ps. 18:35).

Grace is "that which God does for mankind through His Son, which mankind cannot earn, does not deserve, and will never merit. In the Bible the grace of God is described as glorious (Eph. 1:6), abundant (Ac. 4:33), incomparably rich (Eph. 1:7; 2:7), manifold (many-sided, multi-colored, 1 Pe. 4:10) and sufficient (2 Co. 12:9). When we study the concept of grace in the Bible, we notice three things:

1   Grace is part of who God is
2   grace is related to all main doctrines in the Bible
3   grace is to be seen and recognized in the lives of Christians

We will now briefly look at these three aspects.

3. A   Grace is part of who God is

3.A.1   We find the grace of God throughout the Bible

The term 'grace of God' is found twenty times in the New Testament.[4] This phrase expresses the Source of grace. God is called 'the God of all grace' (1 Pe. 5:10), who reigns as sovereign on 'the throne of grace' (Heb. 4:16). The Spirit of God is called 'the Spirit of grace' (Heb. 10:28, 29). The Gospel is called 'the Gospel of God's grace (Ac. 20:24). The Word of God is called 'the Word of His grace' (Ac. 20:32).

The doctrine of divine grace underlies the thought of both the Old and New Testament. However, the Old Testament merely anticipates and prepares for the full expression of grace that becomes manifest in the New Testament. The first use of the word grace in the Bible is in the

---

[4] Lu. 2:40; Ac. 11:23; 13:43; 14:26; 20:24; Ro. 5:15; 1 Cor. 1:4; 3:10; 15:10; 2 Cor. 1:12; 6:1; 8:1; 9:14; Gal. 2:21; Col. 1:6; Tit. 2:11; Heb. 2:9; 12:15; 1 Pe. 4:10; 5:12.

Septuagint translation of Genesis 6:8 where we read that... *"Noah found grace in the eyes of the LORD"*. One of the last words of God in the Bible is on grace: *"He who testifies to these things says, 'Yes, I am coming soon.' Amen. Come, Lord Jesus. The grace of the Lord Jesus be with God's people. Amen."* (Rev. 22:20, 21).

3.A.2   Jesus is the ultimate manifestation of God's grace

The Word became flesh and made his dwelling among us. We have seen his glory, the glory of the One and Only, who came from the Father, full of grace and truth. ... From the fullness of his grace we have all received one blessing after another. For the law was given through Moses; grace and truth came through Jesus Christ. (Jh. 1:14, 16, 17)

Paul, writing to Titus about the first coming of Christ, states "For the grace of God has appeared for the salvation of all men."(Tit. 2:11) The grace of God is more than a divine attribute; it is a divine Person, Jesus Christ. Jesus Christ not only was God incarnate but was grace incarnate. He Himself personifies and expresses the grace of God.

3.B   Grace is related to all main doctrines in the Bible

For it is by grace you have been saved, through faith – and this not from yourselves, it is the gift of God – not by works, so that no one can boast. (Eph. 2:8, 9)

Grace is at the very heart of the Bible, indeed, it is the very foundation. It touches every area of truth or doctrine in one way or another. Every aspect of doctrine is related to grace.

We are declared righteous as a gift by God's grace (Tit. 3:4-8; Ro. 3:21-24). We are saved by grace (2 Ti. 1:9; Ac. 15:8-12). We are forgiven, redeemed, adopted as God's children by grace (Eph. 1:3-8; Ac. 18:26-28). We are called and chosen by grace (2 Tim. 1:7-10; Gal. 1:6; Gal. 1:13-17; Ro. 11:5, 6). Our future hope and eternal security are based on grace (2 Th. 2:15-17; 1 Pt. 1:13-15; Ro. 5:1, 2).

Grace is costly. In his first letter, in which grace is one of his main themes (1:2, 10, 13; 2:19, 20; 3:7; 4:10; 5:10, 12), the Apostle Peter reminds his readers that we are not redeemed with perishable things such as silver and gold, but with "the precious blood of Christ" (1:19).

What an amazing divine paradox – grace was immeasurably costly for God to express and yet is unconditionally free to all men. Grace is God's favor freely offered but expensively expressed!

In 1 Corinthians 15:10, the Apostle Paul writes:

"By the grace of God I am what I am, and his grace to me was not without effect." (1 Co. 15:10).

In this testimony we see an excellent illustration of the practical application of grace. The mark of a child of God is that by the grace of God he is what he is.

3.C   Grace is to be seen and recognized in our lives

"When he (Barnabas) arrived and saw the evidence of the grace of God, he was glad ..." (Ac. 11:23)

Because grace is so much a part of who God is and because it is the basis of our salvation and every good gift of our heavenly Father, it should be normal that grace plays a central role in the lives of Christians and should be seen in all we are and do. When Barnabas arrived in Antioch he **saw** the grace of God in the lives of the believers. The apostles saw the grace of God in Paul, they gave him the right hand of fellowship (Gal. 2:9) Grace is something that is to be seen and recognized in our lives. Grace is sometimes called 'love in action'. Having received it from God and continuing to receive it daily in abundance, it transforms our beings and guides our actions.

Nevertheless, Christians are not always known for their grace.

David Seamond writes:

"The two major causes of most emotional problems among evangelical Christians are the failure to understand, receive, and live out God's

unconditional grace and forgiveness, and the failure to give out that unconditional love, forgiveness, and grace to other people … We read, we hear, we believe a good theology of grace. But that's not the way we live. The good news of the Gospel of grace has not penetrated the level of our emotions."[5]

Therefore it is good to briefly look at what the Bible teaches us about what grace at work in our lives looks like:

3.C.1   Grace empowers us to live changed, godly lives

For the grace of God that brings salvation has appeared to all men. It teaches us to say "No" to ungodliness and worldly passions, and to live self-controlled, upright and godly lives in this present age. (Tit. 2:11, 12)

In these verses and also Titus 3:3-8, Paul makes a clear connection between the doctrine of grace and the lives of Christians. God's grace results in changed lives. Grace brings salvation, but it doesn't stop there, for then grace empowers the believer for daily sanctification. Grace enables us to live differently, to say 'no' to ungodliness and worldly passions, to live self-controlled, upright and godly lives and to do what is good (Tit. 3:8). Christian doctrine is preached most effectively by a Christian's conduct. Creed determines conduct. Grace does not provide the license to do as we please, but the power to do as we ought.

3.C.2   Grace prevents us from becoming bitter and sets us free to forgive and let go

Make every effort to live in peace with all men and to be holy; without holiness no one will see the Lord. See to it that no one misses the grace of God and that no bitter root grows up to cause trouble and defile many. (Heb. 12:14, 15)

---

[5] David A. Seamands, *Healing for Damaged Emotions,* (Scripture Press, Victory Books, USA, 1991), 32.

Grace frees us from a legalistic attitude which always produces a bitterness that defiles many. Legalism puts an emphasis on what we should do for God before what He has done for us in Jesus and puts us (and those around us) in a terrible performance trap. Bitterness inclines a person to harsh and uncharitable opinions of men and things that makes him sour, crabby and repulsive in his general demeanor that brings a scowl over his face and infuses venom into the words of his tongue.

We need grace in our interpersonal relationships, which expresses itself in patience, forgiveness, submission and freedom to allow God to work in that other person. It frees you from trying to be the Holy Spirit in someone else's life. Growing in grace helps us to spend less time and energy critical of and concerned about others' choices, becoming more tolerant and less judgmental.

The poem of an unknown author that Swindoll includes in his book *Grace Awakening* explains that being a person of grace requires letting go of others:

LETTING GO

To let go doesn't mean to stop caring,
it means I can't do it for someone else.
To let go is not to cut myself off.
It's the realization that I can't control another.
To let go is not to enable,
But to allow learning from natural consequences.
To let go is to admit powerlessness,
which means the outcome is not in my hands.
To let go is not to try to change or blame another,
I can only change myself.
To let go is not to care for, but to care about.
To let go is not to fix, but to be supportive.
To let go is not to judge,
but to allow another to be a human being.

To let go is not that I be in the middle arranging all the outcomes,
but to allow others to effect their own outcomes.
To let go is not to be protective,
it is to permit another to face reality.
To let go is not to deny, but to accept.
To let go is not to nag, scold, or argue,
but to search out my own shortcomings and to correct them.
To let go is not to adjust everything to my desires,
but to take each day as it comes.
To let go is not to criticize and regulate anyone,
but to try to become what I dream I can be.
To let go is not to regret the past,
but to grow and live for the future.
To let go is to fear less and love more![6]

3.C.3   Grace reminds us to stay humble

God opposes the proud, but gives grace to the humble (Jas. 4:6; 1 Pe. 5:5; Prov. 3:34)

Humility is both a condition and a result of grace. God's grace helps a believer to understand that in their own natural strength, they cannot walk as God wants, for ultimately this is a supernatural walk, a Spirit-enabled, grace-empowered walk in utter, continual and complete dependence on His sufficient provision.

3.C.4   Grace gives us supernatural strength to deal with difficult circumstances

But he said to me: "My grace is sufficient for you, for my power is made perfect in weakness" (2 Co. 12:9)

---

[6] Charles R. Swindoll, The Grace Awakening, (Milton Keynes, UK: Word Publishing, 1990), 146, 147.

Paul writes that he had been taken up to the third heaven and was given a thorn in his flesh to keep him from exalting himself. Paul entreated the Lord three times to have the thorn removed. In response the Lord said to Paul that His grace is sufficient. If the grace of God is sufficient to save us, surely it is sufficient to keep us and strengthen us in our times of suffering and weakness. God permits us to become weak so that we might receive His strength.

3.C.5   Grace influences the way we speak

Be wise in the way you act toward outsiders; make the most of every opportunity. Let your conversation be always full of grace, seasoned with salt, so that you may know how to answer everyone. (Col. 4:5, 6)

The word 'grace' here refers to actions and words that are pleasant, winsome, courteous, wholesome, sensitive, kind, fitting, gentle, loving, and thoughtful.

Our gracious words reflect the grace of Christ, who uses our graciousness to draw others to His saving grace.

"All spoke well of him and were amazed at the gracious words that came from his lips." (Lu. 4:22)

3.C.6   Grace enables us to give (of) ourselves to others

And now, brothers, we want you to know about the grace that God has given the Macedonian churches. (2 Co. 8:1)

God is able to make all grace abound to you, so that in all things at all times, having all that you need, you will abound in every good work. (2 Co. 9:8)

In 2 Corinthians chapters 8 and 9 the apostle Paul writes about a collection that is being made for the poor Christians in Jerusalem among the churches of the Gentiles. In these chapters, he uses the word 'grace' (charis) 10 times. He uses it as a synonym for Christian giving, which is simply the outflow of the grace of God in and through our lives. If we genuinely understand and appreciate the grace of God extended to sinners such as us, we will want to express that grace by sharing with others. The grace of God will open our heart and our hand, because an open heart cannot maintain a closed hand. Although the context is about financial giving, we can apply it to all other kinds of giving (e.g. time, energy, love, care, and compassion). Because of God's surpassing grace to us, we can be generous in all kinds of ways to others. Believers are channels through whom God's grace can flow to meet the needs of others.

If we look at the importance of grace in the Bible and the lives of Christians, it should not surprise us that the early church reminded each other of the importance of grace. The greeting "Grace and peace to you … etc.," whether as an opening remark or a closing blessing was a common phrase used by Paul and Peter in their letters. (Gal. 1:1; Eph. 1:1; 2 Ti2. 1:1; 1 Pe. 1:2; 2 Pe. 1:2)

To discuss:

In the parable of the Prodigal Son (Luke 15:11-32) Jesus gives us a beautiful illustration of the grace of God ('the father' in the parable) to his children. The parable also shows how difficult it is to live by grace and to share grace with others. Read this parable and discuss the following questions:

1. **How is the grace of the father seen towards:**
   a) his youngest son; b) his oldest son?

2. **What evidence do you find in this parable for the fact that both sons found it hard to receive grace?**

3. **The oldest son wasn't prepared to be gracious to his brother. Do you understand this and do you recognize this attitude in your own life?**

---

4   Developing a grace response to Muslims

We have seen that grace is linked to who God is and all He does and therefore also should be a key characteristic of Christians. Now we want to apply what we learned about grace to our attitude towards Islam and Muslims. Instead of fear, suspicion and prejudice, our response towards Islam and Muslims should be one of grace.

Steve Bell defines a grace-response as follows:

A grace-response is ... "a willingness to alter the default mechanism in our brains which causes us to fear the unfamiliar in another person; being prepared to give others the benefit of the doubt and make an effort to find out why they behave as they do."[7]

A grace response to Muslims consists of the following six elements:

4.1 Apply the Golden Rule

In the Sermon on the Mount Jesus encourages his followers:
"So in everything, do to others what you would have them do to you, for this sums up the Law and the Prophets" (Mt. 7:12).

In obedience to what is often referred to as the 'Golden Rule', in dealing with Islam and Muslims, we should:

1) Judge Islam fairly
When we must evaluate Islam, we should use the same criteria of criticism we want applied to ourselves. We should not compare the worst of Islam with the best of Christianity, e.g., comparing the use of violence by Muslims with the words of Jesus: "I came to bring peace"; or by comparing Muhammad's marriage with the Biblical view on marriage.

2) Be aware of Christianity's past mistakes
In the history of the church, we find many things that have been done in name of Christianity that do not really reflect the truth of the Bible. Being aware of this might make us more gracious towards Muslims, because "people in glass houses should not throw stones".

---

[7] Steve Bell, *Grace for Muslim? The journey from fear to faith,* (Milton Keynes: Authentic Media, 2006), 1.

3) Consider the intent of the Muslim

When examining core issues involving instances in which Islam varies from Christianity, we might ask ourselves what Muhammad's original intention was regarding each point of contradiction and how his view was intended to guide the Muslim. E.g. many Muslims point out that Muhammad's intent was to improve the position of women, as compared with way women were treated in his day and age.

Also, when talking about Muslims in our countries we often assume we know their intentions, instead of asking them about what is intended by their scripture or practice.

4) Refrain from stereotyping

Stereotypes categorize people and reduce complex situations to their simplest forms without subtlety or adequate consideration of the whole picture. Stereotypes depersonalize individuals. We should be careful not to ascribe to all Muslims those opinions or behaviors that are, in fact, only characteristic of some Muslims.

4.2   Loving our Muslim neighbor as we love ourselves

The people of Israel were given guidelines as how to deal with their neighbors, the foreigners in their midst and their enemies. They were told to love their neighbor as themselves (Lv. 19:18); to love the foreigner as themselves (Lv. 19:34) and Jesus encourages His followers to love their enemies (Mt. 5:44). Christians are encouraged to reflect the attitude of God towards their neighbors, foreigners and enemies.

This, among other things, means: We are commanded not to mistreat or oppress them; while we are charged to seek to understand them (Ex. 22:21; 23:9); we are to be kind to them when they are in difficulties (Ex. 23:4, 5); we are to bless them, not take revenge against them and we are to do good to them (Rm. 12:14-21; Pr. 25:21, 22).

4.3   The commandment not to give false testimony about my Muslim neighbor

One of the Ten Commandments is that we should not give false testimony against other people. (Ex. 20:16). Applying this to Islam, it means that when we speak about Islam, we should be seeking to be as truthful as possible. Sometimes fear can lead people to exaggerate situations (e.g. in Numbers 13, the ten spies exaggerated their negative perception of Canaan to discourage the people of Israel from going there). Essentially, Islam is what a Muslim says it is. We should be careful about interpreting the Qur'an and taking verses from it out context, or citing their scriptures without considering how these verses have been or are being interpreted by Muslims scholars. We should be willing to listen to Muslims and to learn to see the world through their eyes.

4.4   A willingness to recognize the positive aspects of Islam

In Genesis 20:1-18 Abraham, who thought that "there would be no one here who fears God", discovers that some people outside the people of Israel (e.g. Abimelech, king of Gerar) had a real reverence for God and were even able to hear and respond to a direct communication from God.

Another aspect of a grace response to Muslims is our willingness to recognize some of the positive aspects of Islam, Muhammad, Islamic civilization, history and culture. We should be open to learning about the positive characteristics of Muslims and Islam. We should be willing to learn from Muslims things that might improve our own relationship with God. We should be looking for traces (echos) of God's grace in Islam. We should be able to appreciate what makes Islam an attractive and reasonable religion in the eyes of millions of people.

4.5   Ability to view Muslims as human beings

The grace of God enables us to view Muslims as human beings with a particular faith, not as representatives of a religious system. It is important that we look beyond the label "veil" to see a mother called

Samira; that we look beyond the term "Muslim" to see Hassan, a hardworking father; that we look beyond the label "Muslim immigrant" to see a young boy or girl Hossaine or Khadija, each of whom has great hopes about their future; that we seek to understand the fears behind the angry, fundamentalist Muslim, Samir A.

Let us seek to find the friend in the Muslim.

4.6   Acknowledge some promises in the Bible that might apply to Muslims

Many Muslims consider themselves descendants of Abraham, through Ishmael. Although it will be hard to prove that this is true for everyone, it seems fair to conclude that it might apply to some Muslims of Arab descent. According to Tony Maalouf in his book *Arabs in the Shadow of Israel,* "older records clearly link ancient north Arabians to Ishmael" and "Ishmael had become a great symbol for north Arabian tribes by the first century AD.".

In light of this it is helpful to keep in mind that God has given his promises to the ancestors of today's Arab Muslims. For example, God promises to bless Ishmael, in response to Abraham's prayer (Gen. 17:20). The election of Isaac (and Israel) does not automatically alienate Ishmael and his descendants from God's spiritual and material care. God deals graciously with Hagar and Ishmael. In Genesis 25:13-18, we have a list of the names of the sons of Ishmael, such as **Nebaoth** and **Kedar**.

The Bible contains several prophetic references to Arab tribes, descendants of Ishmael:

"Sing to the Lord a new song, his praise from the ends of the earth, you who go down to the sea, and all that is in it, you islands, and all who live in them. Let the deserts and its towns raise their voices; let the settlements where **Kedar** *lives rejoice. Let the people of Sela sing for joy … .Let them give glory to the Lord and proclaim his praise … ."(Is. 42:10-12)*

*"Herds of camels will cover your land, young camels of Midian and Ephah. And all from Sheba will come, bearing gold and incense and proclaiming the praise of the Lord. All **Kedar's** flocks will be gathered to you, the rams of **Nebaoth** will serve you; they will be accepted as offerings on my altar, and I will adorn my glorious temple." (Is. 60:6-8)*

According to several early Church Fathers (e.g. Justin Martyr) it is likely that the Magi who came from the East to worship the King of the Jews were Arabs.

> "The gifts presented to the King of the Jews by the magi represented Arabian sources of wealth par excellence. Arabs were the chief producers and conveyors of incense and gold for centuries before Christ. They presented thirty tons of frankincense to the Persian king every year as a token of loyalty. The prophecy of Isaiah 60:1-7 predicted the conversion of the wealth of the nations, primarily of Arabians, to the Messiah in Jerusalem at the dawning of the messianic light upon the nation of Israel. Thus it becomes natural to see Arab magi pledging their allegiance to the King of kings."[8]

The Arab magi might be the first fruit of a harvest to come. God is at work in the Muslim world. Muslims are coming to faith in Christ throughout the world. God reveals Himself to them in dreams and visions. The church is growing in several parts in the Muslim world.

The prophet Isaiah spoke against the land/tribe of **Cush**, which modern scholars identify as an Arabian tribe, probably in what is now northern Sudan. Isaiah speaks of them as "a people tall and smooth-skinned, a people *feared far and wide, an aggressive nation of strange speech, whose land is divided by rivers. (Is. 18:2).*

He concludes his prophecy with a beautiful promise, namely that these same people, who were so greatly feared, will bring gifts to the Lord Almighty, to the place of the Name of the Lord Almighty:

At that time gifts will be brought to the LORD Almighty from a people tall and smooth-skinned, from a people feared far and wide, an ag-

---

[8] Maalouf, 218.

gressive nation of strange speech, whose land is divided by rivers – the gifts will be brought to Mount Zion, the place of the Name of the LORD Almighty. (Is. 18:7)

Can we believe that those who stir up fear in many hearts at the moment, e.g. extreme Muslims, can become people that bring gifts of reverence and respect to the Lord Almighty?

Homework

1. **Read through the parable of the prodigal son (Luke 15:11-32) several times before the next lesson. In which of the three characters (father, younger son, or older brother) do you recognize yourself? How is grace received and given by each of them and in what way do you need to grow more into the likeness of the father, particularly when it comes to being a person who extends grace to others?**

2. **Take the prayer of St. Francis and incorporate it in your prayers in the coming weeks.**

Prayer of St. Francis

Lord, make me an instrument of your peace,
Where there is hatred, let me sow love;
where there is injury, pardon;
where there is doubt, faith;
where there is despair, hope;
where there is darkness, light;
where there is sadness, joy;

O Divine Master, grant that I may not so much seek
to be consoled as to console;
to be understood as to understand;
to be loved as to love.

For it is in giving that we receive;
it is in pardoning that we are pardoned;
and it is in dying that we are born to eternal life.

Background on Francis of Assisi

Francis of Assisi (1182-1226) was an Italian Catholic friar and preacher. He founded the Franciscan Order. When the Crusaders went to the Middle East to fight Muslims with weapons, Francis wandered around various Middle Eastern lands as an apostle of grace. He preached the Gospel to the Sultan, the general of the Muslim armies. Steve Bell describes Francis as "a Christian who balanced political realism with a gracious attitude towards Muslims."[9]

Christine A. Mallouhi in her book Waging Peace on Islam considers Francis an example of how to have contact with Muslims in times of mutual animosity.[10] "It is when the prayer of Francis of Assisi is answered through us that we will find ourselves able to 'bear all things, believe all things, hope all things and endure all things' (1 Cor. 13:7 NKJV). This is a biblical response rather than a human reaction to Muslims."[11]

---

[9] Steve Bell, Grace for Muslims? 5.

[10] To learn more about Francis of Assisi and what we can learn from him in our contact with Muslims, I recommend Waging Peace on Islam by Christine A. Mallouhi, (London, Monarch Books, 2000).

[11] Steve Bell, Grace for Muslims?, 7.

LESSON 3:
UNDERSTANDING MUSLIMS

Aim: to learn about several key aspects of the faith and practice of Islam

1   Introduction

We have examined our attitude and emotions with regard to Islam and Muslims and are beginning to learn to approach Muslims with an attitude of grace. Now we are in a better position to receive accurate information about Islam and Muslims. In the previous lesson we've learned that one aspect of an attitude of grace is to look at Islam through the eyes of Muslims. Therefore the content of this lesson has been assembled using Muslim sources.[12] Also this lesson has been discussed with an imam.

2   Jonah in Islam[13]

In the previous lessons we've looked at the prophet Jonah from a Biblical perspective. In this lesson we want to find out what Islam teaches about Jonah. According to Islamic traditions, the grave of the prophet Jonah (called 'nabi Yunus' in Arabic) is found in present-day Mosul, 400 kilometers north of Bagdad in Iraq. In the so-called Yunus mosque, one can find Jonah's tomb, decorated with whale bones.[14]

A   *References to Jonah in the Qur'an*

The name and/or the story of Jonah is found in the following verses in the Qur'an:

Sura (chapter) 4:163; Sura 10:98-100; Sura 21:87, 88; Sura 37:138-148; Sura 68:48-50.

---

[12] E.g. *Islam: A brief Guide*, The Muslim Educational Trust, UK.
[13] Taken from: http://www.angelfire.com/on/ummiby1/jonah.html and http://etext.virginia.edu/journals/ssr/issues/volume3/number1/ssr03-01-e02.html
[14] The mosque was bombed and destroyed in July 2014 by IS Muslim extremists.

Sura 10 bears his name. In Sura 21:87-90 Jonah is called 'the Fishman' and in Sura 68:48-50 he is called 'the man in the whale'.

So wait with patience for the Command of thy Lord, and be not like the Companion of the Fish – when he cried out in agony. Had not Grace from his Lord reached him, he would indeed have been cast off on the naked shore, in disgrace. Thus did his Lord choose him and make him of the Company of the Righteous (Sura 68:48-50)

And remember Zun-nun, when he departed in wrath: He imagined that We had no power over him! But he cried through the depths of darkness, "There is no god but thou: glory to thee: I was indeed wrong!" So We listened to him: and delivered him from distress: and thus do We deliver those who have faith. (Sura 21:87, 88)

So also was Jonah among those sent (by Us). When he ran away (like a slave from captivity) to the ship (fully) laden. He (agreed to) cast lots, and he was condemned. Then the big Fish did swallow him, and he had done acts worthy of blame. Had it not been that he (repented and) glorified Allah He would certainly have remained inside the Fish till the Day of Resurrection. But We cast him forth on the naked shore in a state of sickness. And We caused to grow, over him, a spreading plant of the gourd kind. And We sent him (on a mission) to a hundred thousand (men) or more and they believed; so We permitted them to enjoy (their life) for a while. (Sura 37:138-148)

Why was there not a single township (among those We warned), which believed, – so its faith should have profited it, – except the people of Jonah? When they believed, We removed from them the penalty of ignominy in the life of the present, and permitted them to enjoy (their life) for a while. If it had been thy Lord's will, they would all have believed, – all who are on earth! wilt thou then compel mankind, against their will, to believe! No soul can believe, except by the will of Allah, and He will place doubt (or obscurity) on those who will not understand. (Sura 10:98-100)

B   Summary of Islamic teaching on Jonah

Based on these verses and also some of the Islamic Traditions (Hadith, writings about what Muhammad said and did), we can summarize Islamic teaching on Jonah as follows:

Jonah was a prophet who was sent by God to his own people in the town of Nineveh. The inhabitants of Nineveh were idolaters who lived a shameless life. Jonah was sent to teach them the worship of Allah. The people disliked his interference in their way of worship, so they argued: "We and our forefathers have worshipped these gods for many years and no harm has come to us." Try as he might to convince them of the foolishness of idolatry and of the goodness of Allah's laws, they ignored him. He warned them that if they kept on with their foolishness, Allah's punishment would soon follow. Instead of fearing Allah, they told Jonah that they were not afraid of his threats. Jonah was disheartened and he left Nineveh, fearing that Allah's anger would soon follow.

Hardly had he left the city when the skies began to change color and looked as if they were on fire. The people were filled with fear by this sight. They recalled the destruction of the people in Noah's time. They all gathered on the mountain and started to beseech Allah for His mercy and forgiveness. Allah's wrath abated and He showered His blessings upon them once again. When the threatening storm was lifted, they prayed for the return of Jonah so that he could guide them.[15] Meanwhile, Jonah had boarded a small ship in the company of other passengers. It sailed all day in calm waters. When night came, the sea suddenly changed. A horrible storm blew as if it were going to split the ship into pieces. The chief crewman asked the crew to lighten the ship's heavy load. They threw their baggage overboard, but this was not enough. Their safety lay in reducing the weight further, so

---

[15] According to Razi in his commentary on the Qur'an, it was on the day of Asjurah (fast day) that the people of Jonah came to change. (In the Jewish synagogue on the fast day on the 9th of the month Av, Tisja Ba'av, during the afternoon prayers, readings are from the book of Jonah).

they decided among themselves to lighten their load by removing at least one person. The captain directed: "We will make lots with all of the travelers' names. The one whose name is drawn will be thrown into the sea." The lot was drawn and "Jonah" appeared. Since they knew him to be the most honorable among them, they did not wish to throw him into the angry sea. Therefore, they decided to draw a second lot. Again Jonah's name was drawn. They gave him a final chance and drew a third lot. Unfortunately for Jonah, his name came up again. The matter was over, and it was decided that Jonah should throw himself into the water. A whale found Jonah floating on the waves before it. It swallowed Jonah into its furious stomach and shut its ivory teeth on him. Three layers of darkness enveloped him, one above the other; the darkness of the whale's stomach, the darkness of the bottom of the sea, the darkness of the night. Jonah prayed to Allah. Allah saw the sincere repentance of Jonah and heard his invocation in the whale's stomach. The whale ejected Jonah onto a remote island. His body was inflamed because of the acids inside the whale's stomach. He was ill, and when the sun rose, its rays burned his inflamed body so that he was on the verge of screaming in pain. However, he endured the pain and continued to repeat his invocation to Allah. Allah caused a vine to grow over him for protection. Then Allah caused Jonah to recover and forgave him. Gradually he regained his strength and found his way to his hometown, Nineveh. He was pleasantly surprised to notice the change that had taken place there. The entire population turned out to welcome him. They informed him that they had turned to believe in Allah. Together they led a prayer of thanksgiving to their Merciful Lord.

C   Jonah in the life of Muslims today

For many Muslims today Jonah is seen as a person they should identify with:

a.   A Muslim student wrote on the internet that if one wants to pass an exam, one should read the prayer of Jonah when he was in the whale.

b.   In responding a question from two Muslim girls as to whether it is allowed to run away from home, a cyber imam writes that running away from home is also a theme found in the Qur'an and he refers to Jonah and writes: "The prophet Yunus tried to run away from his 'home' (which was the place God had called him to be). As a punishment Allah had Yunus eaten by a whale. Yunus spent 40 days in the stomach of the whale. Allah forgave him and Yunus got a second life."

c.   In a sermon of an imam Jonah is given as an example of someone who in the deep darkness was willing to submit (which is what the word "Islam" means in Arabic) to God.

> **To discuss:**
> 1.   **What do you find significant when you compare the Biblical narrative about Jonah with that found in the Qur'an and the Islamic traditions?**
> 2.   **How do you explain the similarities and differences?**

Several aspects of Islam

1   The beginning of Islam

Although Islam as independent religion started in the 6th century AD, according to Muslims the origin of Islam dates back much further. In Sura 3:67 we read: *Abraham was neither a Jew nor a Christian, but he was one inclining toward truth, a Muslim [submitting to Allah]. And he was not of the polytheists.*

The word 'Islam' means 'submission' and a Muslim is 'one who submits' to God. Abraham is considered the Father of the Prophets and many Muslims believe they are descendants of Abraham through his son Ishmael. Ishmael plays an important role in Islamic tradition.

2   The person Muhammad

Muhammad was born in 571 in Mecca (present day Saudi Arabia). His
father died before he was born and his mother died when he was six
years old. When Muhammad was 25 years old he married the widow
Khadija. According to Muslims, when Muhammad was 40 years old he
began receiving revelations from God (Allah). He was convinced he
stood in the footsteps of prophets such as Moses, David and Jesus and
that as the last prophet he, like them, was asked to call people to worship the one and only true God. The people of Mecca used to worship
many gods. Muhammad invited them to Islam (= submission to God).
Several people joined him and became Muslims, while others rejected
him. Gradually the number of followers grew. Initially Muhammad and
his followers faced a lot of opposition from the people in Mecca. And
after 12 years (622 AD) Muhammad and his followers moved to the
city of Yathrib (which later came to be called 'Medina', which means
'city of the prophet'.) That this move is of considerable influence in
Islam is seen from the fact that the Islamic calendar starts from this
event. In Yathrib Muhammad and his followers were received hospi-
tably and shortly after that Muhammad became not just the spiritual
leader, but also the political leader of the city and he founded the first
Muslim state. In the years that followed, the number of followers of
Muhammad grew rapidly. Muhammad, who is described in the Qur'an
as 'a blessing for mankind' (21:107) and 'a good example to follow'
(33:21) died in 632 AD, at age 63. After his death the revelations he
received were collected in a book, the Qur'an. Also his sayings and
examples were collected in a series of books, called the Sunnah.

3   The expansion of Islam

When Muhammad died in 632 AD Muslims lived mostly in Saudi Ara-
bia, but in the years that followed, Islam expanded northwards (to
Syria and Jordan), eastwards (to Iran and Iraq) and westwards (to
Egypt and Algeria). Around 750 AD the whole of North Africa and even
Spain were under Islamic rule. Around 1500 more areas in Africa and
Asia had become Islamic and Indonesia had also become part of the

Islamic world. In the 14th century the Islamic Ottoman Empire started in Turkey. This Empire has had great influence in the Middle East and Central Europe for centuries and has largely contributed to the establishment of Islam in Central and Eastern Europe, e.g. in Albania and Bosnia.

Islam is currently the main religion in forty countries in the world. The Arabs make up about 20 percent of all Muslims. We find many Muslims in Indonesia (196 million), Pakistan (166 million), Bangladesh (150 million), India (150 million), Nigeria (70 million), Turkey (70 million), and Iran (68 million). In Europe (including Russia) there are about 50 million Muslims.

4   What Muslims believe

The doctrines of faith in Islam often contain six articles, namely:

1) Allah (God)
2) Angels
3) The Books of God
4) The prophets
5) The Last Day
6) Predestination

Five of these are mentioned in Sura 2:177 "... *The truly good are those who believe in God and the Last Day, in the angels, the Scripture, and the prophets ...*"

The three fundamental Islamic beliefs are:

a) *Tawhid* – the oneness of Allah
b) *Risalah* – prophethood
c) *Akhirah* – life after death

a   Tawhid

Tawhid is the most important Islamic belief. Muslims believe that everything in existence originates from the one and only Creator, who is the Sustainer and sole Source of Guidance. This belief should govern all aspects of human life. Recognition of this fundamental truth brings a unified view of life which rejects any division into religious and secular. God (Allah) is the sole source of Power and Authority, and is to be worshipped and obeyed. He has no partner; *Tawhid* is pure monotheism. Allah is not born, and He has no son or daughter. Human beings are His subjects. He is the One; He is the Eternal; He is the First and the Last; and there is none like Him. Belief in *Tawhid* brings total change to a Muslim's life. It makes him bow down only to Allah, Who sees all of his actions. He must work to establish the laws of Allah in all areas of his life, in order to gain His pleasure.

b   Risalah

Risalah means prophethood or messengership. Muslims believe that God (Allah) has not left man without Guidance for the conduct of his life. Since the creation of the first man Allah has revealed His guidance to mankind through His prophets. Prophets who received books from Allah are called messengers. All the prophets and messengers came with the same message; they urged the people of their time to obey and worship Allah alone and none other. Whenever the teachings of a prophet were distorted by people, Allah sent another prophet to bring them back to the Straight Path. The chain of *Risalah* began with Adam, included Noah, Abraham, Ishmael, Isaac, Lot, Jacob, Joseph, Moses, David and Jesus, and ended with Muhammad. Muhammad is the final messenger of Allah to mankind. The books containing revelation from Allah are:

The Torah (Tawrat), the Psalms (Zabur), the Gospel (Injil) and the Qur'an. The Qur'an, which was revealed to Prophet Muhammad, is the final book of Guidance.

c   Akhirah

Akhirah means life after death. Belief in *Akhirah* has a profound impact on the life of a Muslim. Muslims believe that we are all accountable to Allah on the Day of Judgment, when we will be judged according to how we have lived our lives. A person who obeys and worships

Allah will be rewarded with a place of happiness in Paradise; the person who does not will be sent to Hell, a place of punishment and suffering. Allah knows our every thought and innermost intention; angels are recording all our actions. If we always keeps in mind that we will be judged by our actions, we will try to make sure that we act according to the Will of Allah. Muslims believe that many of today's problems would disappear if we had this awareness and acted accordingly.

5   Basic religious duties of Islam

Islam has five basic duties, often called the 'pillars of Islam'. Muslims believe that performed regularly, correctly and sincerely these transform a Muslim's life, bringing it into line with the wishes of the Creator. Faithful practice of these duties should inspire a Muslim to work towards the establishment of justice, equality and righteousness in society, and the eradication of injustice, falsehood and evil.

a   Shahadah

Shahadah is the conscious and voluntary declaration of: *La ilaha illallahu Muhammadur rasulullah* "There is no god except Allah, Muhammad is the Messenger of Allah."

This declaration contains the two basic concepts of Tawhid and Risalah.

It is the basis of all actions in Islam; the other four basic duties follow this affirmation.

b   Salah (compulsory prayer)

Salah is offered five times a day, either in congregation or individually. It is a practical demonstration of faith, and keeps a Muslim in constant touch with his Creator. According to Muslims the benefits of *Salah* are far-reaching, long-lasting and immeasurable. *Salah* prepares a Muslim to work towards the establishment of true order in society, and the removal of falsehood, evil and indecency. It develops self-discipline, steadfastness and obedience to the Truth, leading to patience, honesty and truthfulness in the affairs of life.

The five daily prayers are: *Fajr* between dawn and sunrise; *Zuhr* between midday and mid-afternoon; *'Asr* between mid-afternoon and sunset; *Maghrib* just after sunset; *'Isha* between nightfall and dawn.

Muslims believe that five times a day, *Salah* provides a wonderful opportunity to improve one's life. It is considered a system of spiritual, moral and physical training which makes a Muslim truly obedient to his Creator.

c   Zakah (welfare contribution)

Zakah is a compulsory payment from a Muslim's annual savings. It literally means purification, and is an annual payment of 2.5% of the value of cash, jewelry and precious metals; a separate rate applies to animals, crops and mineral wealth. *Zakah* is neither charity nor a tax: charity is optional, whilst taxes can be used for any of society's needs. *Zakah*, however, can only be spent on helping the poor and needy, the disabled, the oppressed, debtors and other welfare purposes, as defined in the Qur'an and Sunnah. *Zakah* is considered an act of worship. It is considered to be one of the fundamental principles of an Islamic economy, which ensures an equitable society where everybody has a right to contribute and share. *Zakah* should be paid with the conscious belief that our wealth and our property belong to Allah, and we merely act as trustees.

d   Sawm (obligatory fast)

Sawm is the annual obligatory fast during the month of Ramadan, the ninth month in the Islamic calendar. From dawn to sunset every day a Muslim refrains from eating, drinking, and smoking and from sex with his marital partner, seeking only the pleasure of Allah. According to Muslims *Sawm* develops a believer's moral and spiritual standards, and keeps him away from selfishness, greed, extravagance and other vices. *Sawm* is considered an annual training program, which increases a Muslim's determination to fulfill his obligations to the Creator and Sustainer.

e   Hajj (pilgrimage to the House of Allah)

Hajj is an annual event, obligatory at least once in a lifetime for Muslims who have the means to perform it. It is a journey to the House of Allah (Al-Kabah) in Mecca, Saudi Arabia, in the month of Dhul Hijjah, the twelfth month of the Islamic calendar. For Muslims *Hajj* symbolizes the unity of mankind; Muslims from every race and nationality assemble in equality and humility to worship God.

According to Muslims, the pilgrim, in the ritual clothing of Ihram, has the unique experience of being in the presence of his Creator, to whom he belongs, and to whom he must return after death.

6   Sources of authority in Islam

The two most important sources of authority that define the faith and religious practice of Muslims are the Qur'an and the Sunnah, while also the various schools of law determine the faith and practice of Muslims.

a   The Qur'an

The Qur'an is the sacred book of Muslims. It is their belief that it is the final Book of Guidance from God (Allah), sent down to Muhammad through the angel Gabriel (Jibra'il). According to Muslims every word of the Qur'an is the Word of Allah. Revealed over a period of 23 years in the Arabic language, it contains 114 chapters (Surahs) and more than 6,000 verses. Muslims learn to recite it in Arabic and many memorize it completely. Muslims are expected to try their best to understand the Qur'an and practice its teachings. Muslims believe that the recording and preservation of the Qur'an is unrivalled. Its teachings cover all aspects of this life and the life after death. It contains principles, doctrines and directions for every sphere of human activity. The theme of the Qur'an broadly consists of three fundamental concepts:

Tawhid, Risalah and Akhirah. According to Muslims, the success of human beings on this Earth and in the life hereafter depends on belief in, and obedience to, the teachings of the Qur'an.

b   The Sunnah

The Sunnah refers to the ways or customs of Muhammad, which means his deeds and sayings and the things as to which he expressed approval. These are contained in the books of *Hadith*, which are collections of his sayings and actions and the actions approved by him, indicating how to put the guidance of the Qur'an into practice. According to Muslims, the Hadith were carefully recorded after Muhammad's death. Six particular collections have become prominent and are regarded as the most authentic: Bukhari, Muslim, Tirmidhi, Abu Dawud, Nasai and Ibn Majah.

The Hadith prescribe matters such as: the times and characteristics of Islamic prayer, rituals for various festivals, how to conduct business in an Islamic way, matters concerning inheritance, wills and testaments; oaths and vows, and instructions for dealing with apostates, etc.

c   Schools of Islamic law (Shari'a)

Sunni Islam acknowledges four schools of law that define religious jurisprudence. These schools are named after their founders:
1) the Hanifi school (mainly in Turkey, the Balkans, Central Asia, India, Pakistan, Bangladesh)
2) the Maliki school (mainly in North Africa)
3) the Shafi'I school (mainly in Yemen, Egypt, Syria, South East Asia and East Africa
4) the Hanbali school (mainly in Saudi Arabia)

The differences among the schools are not in the fundamentals of the Islamic faith, but in finer judgments.

These differences are based on the emphasis put on:

a) the teaching of the Qur'an
b) the Sunnah

c)   consensus of the scholars
d)   similarities with situations in Muhammad's time
e)   common sense

Shari'a is an Arabic word referring to 'a road to a watering place, or well', which is a metaphor for salvation. Constituting the Islamic code of conduct, sharia is derived from four sources:

a)   the precepts set forth in the Qur'an
b)   the example set by Muhammad in the Sunnah
c)   the consensus of religious scholars
d)   an opinion agreed by such scholars upon deliberation based on an analogy (i.e. a comparison with something similar) from the Qur'an and Sunnah.

Muslims differ as to what Shari'a exactly entails. The views held regarding Shari'a vary depending upon whether the believer is a modernist, a traditionalist, a fundamentalist, or an adherent of one of the various schools of Islamic thought and scholarship. And interpretations of Shari'a also vary from one country or culture to another.

The Shari'a contains religious as well as legal norms. It deals with many topics addressed by secular law, including crime, politics, and economics, as well as personal matters such as sexuality, hygiene, diet, prayer and fasting. The fact that many Muslims now live in non-Islamic countries presents a new situation for Islamic law. Among scholars of the Muslim community in Europe discussions are taking place about how to harmonize the demands of Shari'a with European legal systems.

7   Various groups within Islam

The total number of Muslims in the world is about 1.5 billion. Within Islam we can identify several streams. The most important groups are the Sunnis and Shiites. About 80 percent of all Muslims are Sunni. The second largest group (about 15 percent) is Shi'a Muslims.

Shiites are found mainly in Iran and Iraq but also in many other coun-tries. An important distinction between Sunni and Shia Islam is that Shia Muslims acknowledge Ali (the son-in-law of Muhammad) and certain individuals among his descendants (who are known as imams) as the legal heirs of the political and religious leadership within Islam. Many Shiites believe in the infallible imam, an incarnation of the god-head, who is believed to possess supernatural knowledge. They ex-pect the return of the 12th imam, who disappeared in 869 AD, to es-tablish the world domination of Islam.

Within these two main divisions, there are many other smaller sects and groups in Islam, including the Kharijites, the Murji'ites, the Mu'tazilites, the Isma'ili and the Druze. Some of the groups that can be recognized are listed below. Some of groups are not considered real Muslims by other Muslims.

A   Ahmadiyya Muslim Community

The Ahmadiyya Muslim Community (AMC) is a dynamic, fast-growing international revival movement within Islam. The AMC was founded in 1889 by Mirza Ghulam Ahmad (1835-1908), who claimed to have re-ceived divine revelations, and who is considered to be the long-awaited Messiah. Ahmad claimed to be the metaphorical second com-ing of Jesus of Nazareth and the divine guide, whose advent was fore-told by Muhammad. AMC adherents believe that God sent Ahmad, like Jesus, to end religious wars, condemn bloodshed and reinstitute morality, justice and peace. According to his followers, Ahmad divest-ed Islam of fanatical beliefs and practices by vigorously championing Islam's true and essential teachings. The Ahmadiyya Muslim Commu-nity recognizes the teachings of Zoroaster, Abraham, Moses, Jesus, Krishna, Buddha, Confucius, Lao Tzu and Guru Nanak, and believes that their teachings converged into the one true Islam. The AMC, with its headquarters in the UK, claims to have tens of millions of adher-ents worldwide.

B   The Baha'is

The Baha'i community was founded in 1844 in present-day Iran when Ali Muhammad (called 'Baha'u'llah') announced himself to be 'The Gate' (Bab). The essential message of Baha'u'llah was that of unity. He taught that there is only one God, that there is only one human race, and that all the world's religions represent stages in the revelation of God's will and purpose for humanity. The Baha'is believe in the unity of God and mankind, equality between the sexes, harmony of religion and science and an independent search for the truth. They do not consider Muhammad to be the last and greatest prophet, but as one of many. They do not acknowledge the Qur'an as the final revelation, but as one book among many, including the writings of Baha'u'llah'. It is estimated that worldwide there are about 7 million Baha'is. The Baha'i community is often considered to be an apostate Muslim group, and is persecuted in some Islamic countries.

C   The Salafi movement (Wahhabism)

Salafi is a Sunni Islamic movement that takes the pious ancestors (Salaf) of early Islam as exemplary models. The word "Salaf" is an Arabic noun which may be translated as "predecessor" or "ancestor". In Islamic terminology, it is generally used to refer to the first three generations of Muslims. These three generations are looked upon as examples of how Islam should be practiced. The term Salafism is often used interchangeably with "Wahhabism", because Muhammad ibn Abd-al-Wahhab (1703-1787), is considered to be the founder of this movement, although many adherents state that the movement was founded by the prophet Muhammad himself. The Salafi movement is based upon a puritan tradition. They interpret the Qur'an literally and reject everything that is not based upon the original sources of Islam. The Salafi movement has a strong influence in Saudi Arabia and its adherents seek to use their money to spread its teaching and influence around the world.

D   Sufism

Sufism is the mystical stream within Islam. It originated in early Islam. The adherents are called 'Sufis'. The word *Sufi* is often traced to the Arabic word 'Suf' (wool), referring to the simple cloaks the early Muslim ascetics wore. Another suggestion is that the name Sufi comes from the Arabic word 'Safa' (purity), explaining why Sufism emphasized purity of heart and soul. Although Sufis believe in the Qur'an and the Sunnah, they place more emphasis on the inner life and mystical union with God, than on outward obedience to religious duties. According to Sufism the basis of religion is love for God. We have to love God for Who He is, not for any kind of reward, or out of the fear of punishment. God is often addressed as the Eternal Lover. Many Sufis seek mystical union or direct communication with God through dance and music, the recitation of Quranic verses and Islamic poems, through which they seek to achieve an ecstatic state.

E   The Alevis

Around 15 million Muslims are Alevis. They are found predominantly in Turkey, while smaller numbers are found in Syria, Iran and Iraq. It is difficult to make absolute statements about their beliefs and practices, because a wide variety of beliefs and practices prevail among those who call themselves Alevis. There are many similarities between Alevis and the Bektashis of the Balkans.

Alevis are followers of Ali (son-in-law of Muhammad) and believe him to be the successor of Muhammad. Many Alevis equate Muhammad and Ali, and use the single name Muhammed Ali for this personality. Some say Alevism is a mixture of the best elements of Islam, Christianity, Judaism, Manichaeism, Zoroastrianism, Shamanism, and 20th century humanism. Almost all Alevis will deny that God is one who will reward those who follow his rules on earth with eternal pleasures in heaven.

Alevis interpret the Qur'an esoterically, inwardly, or mystically. For them, there are much deeper spiritual truths in the Qu'ran than the strict rules and regulations that appear on the literal surface. Apart from books, perhaps the most important source of Alevi beliefs and thought are the mystical poems and musical ballads that have been passed down from generation to generation, many of which have not been recorded in writing. These poems and ballads are part of the worship meetings, during which adherents seek to enter into a deeper relationship with the spiritual leader of the meeting and with God. The service mainly consists of the leader saying prayers, giving short religious messages, singing solo ballads, and leading the congregation in singing. Another key element is a circling ritual dance performed by selected men and women in a group that can vary in size. The service is held entirely in Turkish, including all the prayers and singing.

Alevis do not accept the idea of a hard-faced God judging man based on how he has performed his religious duties during his life on earth. Alevis tend not to practice the prayers five times a day, nor the observance of fasting during the month of Ramadan. Instead they keep a 12-day fast during the first month of the Muslim calendar. Visiting Mecca is not an Alevi practice. However, visiting and praying at the tombs of Alevi-Bektashi saints is quite common. Alevi women worship together with men, Alevi women are free to dress in modern clothing.

F   Folk Islam

Although not really a stream within Islam, we cannot ignore the importance of so-called Folk Islam. In the daily life of many Muslims, orthodox convictions go hand in hand with practices which probably have their origin in pre-Islamic times. Such practices involve customs regarding birth, puberty, marriage and funerals etc., as well as practices relating to protection against misfortune (Muslims sometimes refer to the so-called "evil eye"). When a woman is barren, sometimes one seeks help in the form of intercession from Muslim saints who have died. Also, dreams, predictions, blessings and curses play an important role in the daily life of many traditional Muslims.

8   Islamic culture and customs

When we want to develop a good relationship with Muslims it is important to know something of the Islamic culture and customs. Of course, it is not possible to briefly describe the culture and customs of all Muslims in our country. There are many differences and it is important that through conversation we learn about our Muslim friend's own cultural background and customs. May it suffice that we mention below some things to which many Muslims would adhere:

A   The Islamic calendar

The Islamic calendar starts with the year 622 AD. The Islamic year consists of 12 lunar months. The lunar year is about 11 days shorter than our solar year. The exact dates on which festivals (and also the month of fasting (Ramadan) starts, can often only be established at the last moment, because it is dependent upon the appearance of the moon. For example, the year 2014 AD is the year 1435-1436 AH (Anno Hijrah, the year Muhammad fled from Mecca to Medina).

B   Islamic Festivals

Muslims state they observe festivals not for their own pleasure in them, but to seek the pleasure of God (Allah). They are, however, occasions of joy and happiness. The two major festivals in Islam are *'Id ul Fitr* and *'Id ul Adha*.

'Id ul Fitr falls on the first day after the month of Ramadan. On this day, after a month of fasting, Muslims offer congregational prayer, preferably on open ground. They express their gratitude to Allah for enabling them to observe the fast. Special food is prepared. It is customary to visit friends and relatives, and to make the occasion special for children.

'Id ul Adha begins on the 10th day of the month of Dhul Hijjah and continues until the 13th. This celebration commemorates the willingness Abraham displayed when he was asked to sacrifice his own son, Ishmael. Abraham showed his readiness and Allah was very pleased.

At the command of Allah, a ram was sacrificed instead of Ishmael. Muslims offer congregational prayer on the day of this commemoration, and they sacrifice animals such as sheep, goats, cows and camels. The meat of the sacrificed animal is shared amongst relatives, neighbors and the poor.

Other celebrations include the *Hijrah* (migration of the Prophet), *Lailatul Miraj* (Night of the Ascension) and the dates of Islamic battles. There is a special night called *Lailatul Qadr* (Night of Power), an odd-numbered night in the last ten days of Ramadan. The Qur'an says it is "better than a thousand months". Muslims spend the night offering prayers and reciting the Qur'an.

C   Diet

Muslims are encouraged in the Qur'an to eat what is good and wholesome for them, and are forbidden to eat certain foods. A Muslim is not allowed to eat: a) pigs; b) animals not slaughtered in the name of Allah; c) the blood of animals; d) carnivorous animals.

Fish and vegetables are permitted. Islamic law requires animals to be humanely slaughtered by a sharp knife penetrating the inner pad of the neck, to allow maximum drainage of blood. The name of Allah must be said at the time of slaughter. All alcoholic drinks are prohibited.

D   Dress

Muslims are encouraged to dress modestly and decently. No particular dress is recommended. The requirements include:

- For men, covering at least from the navel to the knees;
- For women, covering the whole body except the face and hands; according to some scholars, women above the age of puberty should cover their faces when going out or meeting strangers;
- Men and women must not dress in a manner that arouses sexual feelings, e.g. by wearing clothing that is transparent, skin-tight or exposes half of the body;
- Men are not allowed to wear pure silk or gold;

- Men must not wear women's clothes, and vice-versa;
- Wearing of the symbolic dress from other religions is not allowed.
- Simplicity and modesty are encouraged. Dress expressing arrogance is disliked. The style of dress depends on local custom and climate.

To discuss:
1. **Are there things Christians can learn from Muslims? If so, what?**
2. **Mention several similarities and differences between Muslims and Christians?**

---

9 The main problems Muslims have with Christians/the Christian faith

When Christians start relating to Muslims, they often discover that there are several things that Muslims find hard to understand or accept about Christians and the Christian faith. We can summarize the main things in three categories:

a)   our faith
b)   our history
c)   our morals

a   *Our faith*

Muslims do not understand our conception of the Trinity and are convinced that Christians believe in three gods. As we have seen before, Muslims strongly emphasize the unity of God and they consider every deviation from this unity to be a very serious offence.

Although Muslims have a lot of respect for Jesus and acknowledge Him as an important prophet, they do not understand how Christians can speak of Jesus as 'the Son of God'. They think that when Christians say this they believe that God the Father had a sexual relationship with Mary and that Jesus was born as a result of this. This thought is very offensive to a Muslim.

Because God is almighty and Jesus is one of the prophets He sent to the world, Muslims cannot understand that God allowed Jesus to be treated so disgracefully as to be killed by crucifixion. The Qur'an states that God took Jesus into heaven just before people tried to crucify Him and that God had someone who looked like Jesus take the place of Jesus on the cross and suffer and die in his stead.

Many Muslims do not understand how Christians can believe in the infallibility of the Bible. This is because Christians use a variety of Bible translations, and because as they see it, Christians cannot adequately explain what appear to Muslims to be contradictions found in the Bible.

b   _Our history_

In the Middle Ages "Christian" armies went to the Holy Land to cleanse the region from "unchristian" influences. In doing so, they killed thousands of people (including many Muslims). Muslims some-times consider these Crusades to be the Christian version of "jihad" (holy war).

From the 17th till the 20th century several "Christian" countries (e.g. Spain, Portugal, England, France and the Netherlands) were colonial powers who dominated parts of the world (where many Muslims lived), using violence, robbery, lies and exploitation.
Muslims often don't understand why many Christians give uncondi-tional support to Israel, a country that sometimes uses violence to accomplish its goals.

Many Muslims believe that the people in the Western world (often used as a synonym for Christianity) often behave as they were cultur-ally, politically and economically superior to the rest of the world, and that furthermore, the West lacks the willingness to learn from the richness of other cultures and countries.

c   *Our morals*

While the Western world (in the eyes of many Muslims) behaves like a policeman who seeks to make the rest of the world abide by its law, the West seems blind to the moral decay that goes on in Western societies. To Muslims this decay seems obvious in the acceptance of homosexuality, the legalization of drugs and prostitution, the practice of abortion and euthanasia, the high rate of divorce, the prevalence of domestic violence, and the spread of immorality by means of films and tourism.

To discuss:
1.   **What is your first reaction to how Muslims view Christians and Christianity?**
2.   **How can we respond to the way we are perceived by Muslims?**

Homework

Write down at least two questions that you would like to ask the Muslims who you will be meeting in the mosque during the next lesson.

LESSON 4:
MEETING WITH MUSLIMS

Aim: to meet with Muslims and ask them about their faith and how they practice their faith

Now that we have looked at our attitude towards Islam and Muslims and learned about some important aspects of the faith and life of Muslims, it is time to meet with Muslims and interact with them about their faith. We have learned that one of the characteristics of an attitude of grace is to see Islam through the eyes of Muslims and abstain from making a caricature of Muslims.

The best way to learn about what Muslims believe, think and do is to ask them directly. It has been our experience that Muslims are more than willing to meet with Christians and talk with them about their faith and also listen to what Christians believe. Therefore we would like to use lesson 4 to visit a local mosque and interact with the Muslims there.

When visiting the mosque, keep the following in mind:

1. Wear modest conservative clothing which exposes a minimum of flesh (e.g. no shorts or sleeveless shirts on either men or women). Women should wear a headscarf and a dress, or a blouse and a skirt (at least to the knees). It is preferable that sleeves be elbow-length or longer. Men should wear long trousers and a shirt with sleeves. Often women are asked to cover their heads while in the mosque. You can bring your own shawl, otherwise one will be provided for you.

2. It is common that you will be asked to remove your shoes when entering the mosque.

3. Prepare in advance some questions you would like to ask.

4. Be courteous and respectful at all times, even when you hear or see things with which you are totally in disagreement or in

the event that someone seems to be trying to convert you to Islam. It is very likely that your hosts will present the truth in a rather overly optimistic way, but realize that this is what you yourself would also do in the event that a group of Muslims were to visit your church.

5. If you are asked about the Christian faith, try to give a reply that reflects as much as possible your personal experience of your faith. So instead of saying "Christians think prayer is very important", you could explain how you personally pray daily.

6. The goal of this visit is not to convert your Muslim hosts, but to learn from them. But, when you have the opportunity to re-spectfully share about your faith in the Lord Jesus Christ, by all means do so.

Assignment after your visit to the mosque

1. **What is the most significant thing you learned from your visit to the mosque?**
2. **Read Acts 10 and think about the relationship between Cornelius and Peter. Compare Cornelius with the Muslims you have met:**
   a. **Do you think that God hears the prayers of these Muslims? What do you think happens when they pray?**
   b. **Peter learned an important lesson from Cornelius. What have you learned from the Muslims you met?**
   c. **What do you like most about the faith of Muslims?**
   d. **Cornelius needed only one vision to take action. Peter needed three. Do you know of other examples that indicate Christians may be less receptive to what God has to say than people outside the church?**

LESSON 5:
BUILDING RELATIONSHIPS THAT LAST

Aim: to learn to be a relational witness and share your life with Muslims

> **To do:**
> **Discuss your visit to the mosque and the assignments completed afterwards.**

Now we have discussed our attitude towards Muslims and Islam and learned more about the faith and lives of Muslims and also have had an opportunity to meet with Muslims. It is time to consider how we can share our lives with Muslims, and in this context, talk with them about our faith in Jesus Christ. This is the subject of our fifth and final lesson of this course.

A   Jesus' incarnation: a model for us

In John 1:14 we read that *"The Word became flesh and made his dwelling among us."* This refers to the incarnation of Jesus, which is the model par excellence for the ministry of Christians in this world. We should follow Jesus' example. He adopted a servant's identity and became part of a community (Philippians 2:5-8). The Apostle Paul in 1 Corinthians 9:19-23 shows that he was willing to make himself a slave to everyone, in order to win as many as possible.
Commenting about his ministry in Thessalonica, he writes:

"We loved you so much that we were delighted to share with you not only the gospel of God, but our lives as well, because you had become so dear to us."(1 Thess. 2:8)

This verse reflects the way the Apostle Paul ministered in the city of Thessalonica. He and his team had a genuine love for the people with whom they shared the Gospel. They did not merely deliver a message, but also gave of themselves.

"The true missionary is not someone specialized in the delivery of the message but someone whose whole being, completely committed to a message which demands all, is communicated to his hearers."[16]

In this letter Paul mentions nine times 'you know', referring to the fact that the people of Thessalonica had observed his life from close by.

We need to integrate proclamation and incarnation. An important concept in the Bible is that of the Kingdom of God. God's master plan of redemption is that God may glorify Himself by uniting all things under Christ. This includes not only the reconciliation of people to God, but the reconciliation of "all things in heaven and on earth" (Eph. 1:10). This reconciliation finds its final fulfillment in the future Kingdom of God, but glimpses of this future Kingdom can be seen in the present. The church is not just to proclaim the Gospel of the Kingdom (Matt 24:14), but also to display the life of the Kingdom (Matt 5-7) and to perform the works of the Kingdom.

When applying the above to our relationships with Muslims, we can learn five things:

a   Evangelism is first of all a lifestyle, not an activity; it is not something we do, but something we are.

b   Verbal sharing of the Gospel needs to be integrated in one's life and needs to be linked with addressing social needs that are a result of a broken relationship with the Lord.

c   The life of the believer needs to be in agreement with the content of His message.

d   In order for Muslims to have an accurate understanding of Jesus Christ and Biblical faith, they need to see an expression of it in the lives of people they know and trust.

e   In order for Christians to be an incarnation of the truth of the Gospel in the lives of Muslims, they need to have an accurate

[16] Ernest Best, Black's New Testament Commentaries, ed., A commentary of the First and Second Epistles to the Thessalonians (Peabody, Massachusetts: Hendrickson Publishers, 1993), 102, 103.

understanding of their Muslim friends in the context of a relationship of love and trust.

This means there needs to be close proximity between Christians and
Muslims.

> **To discuss:**
> a   **What would it be like if every Muslim in your country were
>   to have at least one Christian friend?**
> b   **What does it mean to be an incarnational or relational wit-
>   ness?**

*"What makes us different is not simply what we believe, but how our
beliefs motivate and affect our behavior. What makes us different is
how our faith transforms the way we live … Unless we … learn to
demonstrate that dynamic and transforming relationship between our
beliefs and our behavior we are in no better position than any other
faith "*[17]

Although the theology of the Christian faith is different from the theology of Islam, the vast majority of Muslims will only know that it is
different when it affects how we behave.

We've seen earlier in this course that Jonah's theology did not affect
his behavior. He might have been able to have a discussion on the
concept of grace and forgiveness with the people in Nineveh, but he
was not willing to show this grace to them through his life.

Merely discussing our beliefs seldom convinces people of the truth of
them. What makes a difference is when Muslims see our beliefs put
into practice.

Mostly Jesus did not argue with the rulers of his time about the validi-
ty of the kingdom of God; he went about demonstrating the kingdom

---

[17] Richard Sudworth, *Distinctly Welcoming*, (NSW Australia: Scripture Union Australia, 2007), 48.

of God and explaining how to understand it and live it. We need to do the same.

Incarnational or relational witness is also referred to as friendship evangelism. It is a relational or personal approach: working mainly one-on-one (or with one family) rather than in a group setting, building a relationship. Witnessing about our faith to Muslims should ideally be incorporated into a relationship of love, trust and respect. It takes time to develop such a relationship and it goes far beyond a one-time discussion with a stranger about the Christian faith and Islam. Among other things, it means doing things together, spending time together, developing an interest in each other's lives, sharing our joys and grief, becoming good friends in the full sense of the word.

It means sharing your whole life and not just sharing the Gospel.

Our sincere concern and care provides us with plenty of opportunities to share Biblical truths. Not in an abstract way, void of relational connection, but as part of our daily life. In natural and everyday scenes you can live out your faith before your Muslim friends, both in word and in deed. There will be exchanges in conversation in which you can express Christian truths and pray with or for your friend. Also, they will see you practicing your faith (e.g. fasting, celebrating Christmas, or how you deal with conflict, how you handle money, how you relate to your family, etc.).

Our Muslim friends will observe in our daily living the saving work and power of Jesus. Most Muslims come to a true appreciation of the gospel and desire for our Lord by seeing Christian faith lived out in the daily struggles of real Christians, serving openly, humbly, faithfully, by their sides in their communities.

Confrontation may occur when difficult questions are asked, but as friends we know how to disagree in the appropriate manner.

Incarnational witness can be costly and painful, as we also see in Jesus' life of suffering and even death.

How often you will be given an opportunity to share about the Gospel cannot be programmed. Yet in our concern for people who have not heard about Christ, you will, of course, be praying for God to help you know when to speak, when to listen, and how to be sensitive to your friend's needs and beliefs. Also, you will learn to become more out-spoken about your own faith and become more explicit in pointing out how God relates to the choices you make, the responses you give, etc.

In the Bible we read about Andrew bringing his brother Peter to meet Jesus, and Philip bringing his friend Nathanael to Jesus. Evangelism is sometimes described as bringing our friends to meet our best Friend: Jesus. Being a relational witness, we want to have our Muslim friends meet Jesus our best Friend so that each of them might choose to bow to His Lordship and become his friend too.

To discuss:

1   "Just arguing about beliefs rarely convinces people of the va-
     lidity of them. Seeing them in action makes the difference."
     Explain why you agree or disagree with this statement.

2   In 1 Corinthians 9:19-23 Paul explains that he made himself a
     slave to everyone to win as many as possible. How can we
     apply this principle in our relationships with Muslims?

B   Practical ways to connect naturally with Muslims

In Jesus' time Jews and Samaritans lived in the same country, but we read "Jews do not associate with Samaritans" (John 4:9). We might say the same thing about Muslims and Christians in our country, city or street. Perhaps this course has encouraged you to start sharing your life with a Muslim. But then your question might be: how and where do I start?

Therefore, we would like to give you some practical suggestions as to how to start building relationships with Muslims:

1   Offer yourself as a volunteer in the local community, or refugee, immigration center.

2   Contact your local mosque or Islamic center in order to have a meeting to get to know them, ask whether there is something you can do for them or whether there are activities in which you or your church can work together with them. You can also invite them for a meeting in your church.

3   Together with your Muslim neighbors organize a fun-night with food, clothing, and music from different cultures to get to know each other's culture better.

4   Ask Muslims in your neighborhood for specific prayer requests and start praying for them.

5   Learn basic vernacular greetings and expressions (e.g. in Arabic, Turkish or any other language spoken by Muslims in your city) and start greeting them on the street.

6   Around Easter or Christmas prepare special gifts to hand out to the Muslims in the neighborhood to celebrate this feast with them.

7   Use their business services (e.g. shop in a Moroccan bakery or Turkish grocery store or have your hair done by an Islamic hairdresser) and start talking to the people there.

8   Find out what specific social needs there are among the Muslims in your neighborhood and start offering courses/classes to meet such needs (e.g. language classes, sports activities, homework classes, sewing or computer lessons, etc.).

9   Participate in activities that are geared towards Muslim immigrants in your town or city.

10 Sit next to them in a bus or metro and start a conversation.

11 Seek ways to collaborate with them in community projects.

12 Seek ways to help your Muslim neighbors in a practical way.

13 Visit an Islamic website chatroom and chat with them.

14 Join them when they sit together in the local park.

This is by no means an exhaustive list, but just a few examples, which could be complemented by many others. The main idea is to find ways to naturally connect with the Muslims in your city, street, apartment block, etc.

C   Some Do's and Don'ts in relationships with Muslims

As was pointed out earlier, the most effective Christian witness arises naturally out of situations in which Christians and Muslims meet together. It is impossible to learn in advance what to do and what to say, how to respond and behave in each and every situation that occurs. Nevertheless, we can give some general guidelines:

i   Beware of the differences between the sexes (e.g. for a man it might be improper to shake hands with a woman, or visit a home when only the woman is at home).

ii   Use your Bible with respect (no underlining, no stickers, don't place it on the floor).

iii   Never offer your Muslim friends pork or alcohol. Strict Muslims will only eat meat that is halal, i.e. killed by a Muslim following the proper ritual and using the name of Allah.

iv   Pray regularly for your Muslim friend(s). If you want you can ask them for specific prayer requests.

v   Be prepared to speak about anything (not just religious subjects) and be open about your faith; make connections between your faith and your daily life.

vi   Do not attack Islam, Islamic practices, Muhammad. Be careful to avoid criticizing Islam. Jesus teaches us to not look at the speck of sawdust in someone else's eye while ignoring the plank in our own eye (Mt. 7:1-5). We don't become white by painting others black.

vii   Don't start an argument (consider the warning of Paul in 2 Tim. 2:23, 24 about foolish and stupid arguments).

viii When in disagreement, don't force the issues, leave the door open for the next visit/opportunity/conversation.

ix   Do all you can to remove misunderstandings about the Christian faith, and be prepared to admit the mistakes and crimes of Christians in the past and the present.

x   To explain Biblical truth use stories, examples and your personal testimony (not only how you came to faith, but also how the Lord answered your prayer, gave you a comforting verse, or guided you recently, etc.). Better to say: "I believe that ... or "It is my conviction that ..." or "I believe the Bible teaches that ..." instead of the more generic: "The Bible teaches that ..." or "Christianity believes that ..."

xi   Walk the talk. The hardest and most significant part of evangelism is being an example and an illustration of the verbal message we share.

xii   Be yourself. This is the easiest to keep up over a long period of time.

D   A model of meeting

"After three days they found Him in the temple courts, <u>sitting among the teachers</u>, <u>listening to them</u>, and <u>asking them questions</u>. Everyone who heard Him was amazed at his <u>understanding</u> and his <u>answers</u>." (Luke 2:46, 47)

We are called to be like Christ in relationships. The above verses are taken from Luke's account of Jesus, at the age of 12 in the temple. Colin Chapman sees in this episode a good model of a genuine meeting with Muslims and he points out the following five details:[18]

<u>Sit among them</u>.
Jesus sat among the teachers. How can Christians sit among Muslims? By visiting them in their homes, spending time with them socially, visiting a mosque, an Islamic youth center or student group, etc. We have to look for natural ways of connecting. How much do we know about the community to which they belong or about their history and

---

[18] Colin Chapman, *Cross and Crescent: responding to the Challenge of Islam* (Downers Grove, II., USA: IVP Books, 2007), 24, 25.

culture? Do we know what it feels like to be in their shoes? Am I aware of how they react to me as a person?

Listen

Jesus listened to the teachers. How can Christians learn to listen to Muslims? Through having a sincere desire to learn what they think. By giving serious attention to how they themselves express their faith, instead of only paying attention to what is being said about them in the media. It means that we learn about their world, their background. That we learn to stand in their shoes and see the world through their eyes. It means that we learn to listen with our hearts and not just with our ears. The Bible makes clear that "the person who listens well, will testify successfully" (Proverbs 21:28).

Ask questions

Jesus asked questions. When we have taken the first two steps, we are in a better position to ask good questions without Muslims considering such questions to be a threat. We could begin with basic questions, but could be more probing, questioning gently some of their beliefs and statements. We do not ask questions to embarrass our Muslim friend, but to really enter into a conversation.

Understand

The teachers saw that Jesus understood them. The answers to our questions will lead us to a better understanding of Islam in the life of our Muslim friend, not as we read it in a book. Understanding also enables us to discern the most important issues and not get side-tracked into fruitless discussions.

Answer

Jesus answered the questions posed by the teachers. When Muslims see we really understand them, they might begin asking questions about our faith. Once we reach the stage of being able to offer any answers, we will then be answering genuine questions in the minds of Muslims and not simply the questions that we think they ought to be asking. At this stage we've also earned the right to speak.

> Ask the Lord to bring you in contact with at least one Muslim with whom you can start building a meaningful relationship in order to be His witness in their lives.

Conclusion

The course "Sharing Lives" is over. For more questions and additional information and next steps, you can get in write to: info@sharinglives.eu

For books, DVD's and addresses to obtain additional information, refer to the appendix below and check on the website: www.sharinglives.eu .

APPENDIX

Resources for those who want to learn more[19]

There are a growing number of good books and DVDs to help you understand your Muslim friends better and to share your life, and in this context, also our faith with them. Some examples are set forth below.

Inside Islam (DVD)

"Inside Islam" is a 2002 documentary that provides a good introduction to Islam. Topics include Islam's connections with Judaism and Christianity, the life of Muhammad, the Five Pillars of Islam (the profession of faith, prayer, charity, fasting during Ramadan, and the pilgrimage to Mecca), and the history of Islam, women in Islam, European colonialism, Islamism, the Nation of Islam and jihad.

Cross and Crescent: responding to the challenge of Islam
Colin Chapman

Challenging us to examine our own attitudes, Colin Chapman considers the issues involved in Christian engagement with Muslims and Islam. He explores, ultimately, how Christians can effectively bear witness to Jesus. This book includes material on 'Islamic Terrorism', 'What is Islam?', 'The Qur'anic View of Christians' and 'Explaining Christian Beliefs About Jesus'. It will equip Christians to better understand Muslims and Islam in a rapidly-changing world.

---

[19] Recommending these materials doesn't mean we agree with all content found there.

Grace for Muslims? The journey from fear to faith
Steve Bell

Why should an essentially 'benign' religion turn some into 'demons'?" asked a Muslim journalist. It is a question that is at the heart of the Islamic debate. Alarmist claims are made about these 'demons', while the possibility of a peaceful Islam is dismissed. Many are confused about the religion's contradictory faces. Is it possible for Christians to relate to Muslims without being politically naive or theologically liberal? Steve believes it is. He shares his own journey and reflects upon how he arrived at the crucial ingredient – grace.

Encountering the world of Islam
Keith Swartley (editor)

"Encountering the World of Islam" is a textbook, including articles from eighty authors who have lived throughout the Muslim world. This book guides you on a journey into the lives of Muslims around the world and in your neighborhood. Through this comprehensive collection, you will learn about Muhammad and the history of Islam, gain insight into today's conflicts, and dispel western fears and myths. You will also discover the frustrations and desires of Muslims and learn how to pray for and befriend them. Encountering the World of Islam provides a positive, balanced, and biblical perspective on God's heart for Muslims and equips you to reach out to them in Christ's love.

The Crescent through the Eyes of the Cross
Nabeel T. Jabbour

In this book, the author (an Arab Christian) seeks to help readers understand and develop compassion for Muslims by means of a fictional account about Ahmad, one of his Muslim friends. We also 'hear' from Ahmad's father and sister in Egypt. Through 'the mouth' of Ahmad and his relatives the author discusses several aspects of the Muslim worldview, which Christians who want to share the Good News need to understand, such as: the relationship between Jesus Christ, Mohammad, the Qur'an and the Bible; the role of Israel, cultural differences; the role of women, the Western 'Christian' history of the Crusades and Colonialism; contextualizing our message; and integrating people with a Muslim background into the Church.

Waging Peace on Islam
Christine A. Mallouhi

How can caring Christians approach Islam? As relations between Islam and the West grow more polarized, many Christians are nervous about meeting Muslims. How can we possibly overcome years, if not centuries, of mistrust? Christine Mallouhi, who married into a Muslim family and has lived much of her life in the Middle East, suggests we should emulate St. Francis, who during the Crusades went to be with the Muslims and even shared the gospel with the Sultan.

The Costly Call
Emir Fethi Caner and H. Edward Pruitt

Twenty modern-day stories of Muslims from different parts of the world, who found Jesus.

Daughters of Islam – Building Bridges with Muslim Women
M. Adeney

In Daughters of Islam, Miriam Adeney introduces you to women like Ladan, Khadija and Fatma. You'll learn about their lives, questions and hopes. You'll learn how they are both representative of and unique among their Arab, Iranian, Southeast Asian and African sisters. And you'll discover what has drawn them to Christ. As you enter into the lives of Ladan, Khadija and Fatma, you'll gain insight into how to relate to other women of Muslim background – and how to introduce them to Christ.

The World of Islam (CD)

The World of Islam CD-ROM contains 39 complete books and numerous articles on Islam and Christian witness, including a 750-page Dictionary of Islam, articles regarding contextualization and the roots of fundamentalism and militancy in Islam. Ten newly updated maps depict the current situation of the Muslim world. In addition, over 100 printable photographs of the Islamic world, eight complete courses of study on Islam by noted scholars, a complete, searchable text of the Qur'an, an annotated bibliography, links to Web sites related to Islam and much more ... over 12,000 pages of resources!

More than dreams (DVD)

In a docu-drama format this DVD contains five true-life stories of former Muslims who now know Jesus as their Savior. Stories were selected from Egypt, Iran, Turkey, Nigeria, and Indonesia. More Than Dreams re-created each of these stories, producing each in its original language. The movies include a ministry segment explaining what it means to follow Christ and leading viewers in the salvation prayer.

Bert de Ruiter (ed.)

Engaging with Muslims in Europe

In Europe one finds Christian communities and
Muslim communities living in close proximity to
each other. Muslims and Christians pass each
other in the streets, stand next to each other
waiting for the bus or metro, live next to one
another in streets, share apartment buildings
with each other, study in the same universities,
have their lunches in the same business
canteens, shop in the same shopping centres.
Nevertheless, they are essentially strangers to
each other. Only a small minority of Churches and Christians in Europe
are engaged with Muslims through meaningful and loving relationships
which provide opportunities to witness to them about the truth of God.

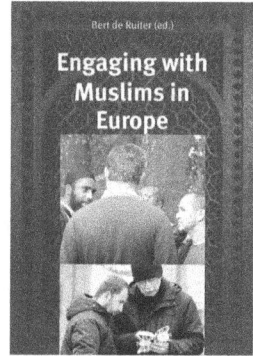

The European Ministry to Muslims Network of the European Leadership
Forum seeks to equip the Church in Europe to relate to Muslims with a
compassionate heart, an informed mind, an involved hand and a
witnessing tongue. In this book members of the network and others
write about their engagement with Muslims in Europe.

Pb. • pp. 112 • £ 7.00 • € 8.00
ISBN 978-3-95776-025-8

VTR Publications • Gogolstr. 33 • 90475 Nürnberg • Germany
info@vtr-online.com • http://www.vtr-online.com

Bert de Ruiter

Sharing Lives
Overcoming Our Fear of Islam

This book argues that the single greatest hindrance to Christian witness amongst Muslims in Europe is fear.

Many European Christians fear that Europe will gradually turn into Eurabia, or Islamic domination of Europe, and they ignore the efforts of Muslims to adapt to the European context, a situation pointing to a future scenario of Euro-Islam, or Islam being Europeanized. The author argues that instead of an attitude of fear, which leads to exclusion, Christians should develop an attitude of grace, which leads to embrace.

After analyzing books and courses developed to help Christians relate to Muslims, he concludes that these mostly concentrate on providing information and skills, instead of dealing with one's attitude. Because of this the author developed a short course to help Christians overcome their fear of Islam and Muslims and to encourage Christians to share their lives with Muslims and to share the truth of the Gospel.

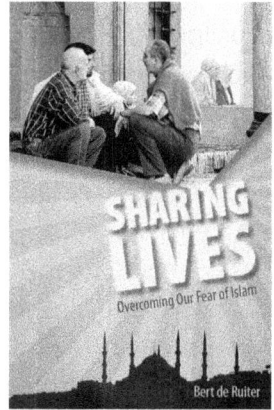

Pb. • pp. XIII + 209 • £ 13.95 • € 14.90
ISBN 978-3-941750-22-7

VTR Publications • Gogolstr. 33 • 90475 Nürnberg • Germany
info@vtr-online.com • http://www.vtr-online.com

www.ingramcontent.com/pod-product-compliance
Lightning Source LLC
Chambersburg PA
CBHW072013060426

42446CB00043B/2426